The things they say...

"It's easy to do good – if many people help."
(plaque on the wall of the first-ever SOS family house at Imst, Austria)

- Hermann Gmeiner, founder of the SOS Children's Villages organisation

"You can do it in a Daewoo."
(slogan for the Challenge, dreamed up in the bath)

- Richard Meredith, author of Which Way Next?

"What time will the 8 o'clock train arrive?"
(illustration of time-keeping attitudes in Bangladesh)

- Theo Gomes, director of the national SOS Children's Village Association, Dhaka.

About the author

Richard Meredith is an author, writer and journalist whose background has been mainly in newspapers and the business press. He is an elected member of the Society of Authors and his previously published works have included *One Way or Another* in the 'Balding Backpacker' series (ISBN 0-9541432-0-5) and *Voice From the Front Lines*, a collection of articles about the UK publishing industry (ISBN 0-9541432-1-3). When not travelling he lives sometimes in Spain, but mostly at a century-old, former farm-worker's cottage in England with a pub at the end of the lane.

Which Way Next?

*Story of the Daewoo Challenge
- an epic journey from the UK to
South Korea in a family hatchback*

RICHARD MEREDITH
The 'Balding Backpacker'

MercuryBooks

Which Way Next?

· · · · · · · · · · · · ·

Published by Mercury Books, PO Box 3620, MK16 0XQ, England
Web: www.mercurybooks.co.uk   E: mercurybooks@btconnect.com

The right of Richard Meredith to be identified as the author of this work has been asserted by him in accordance with the Copyright, Designs and Patents Act, 1988.

Published as a Special Edition by Mercury Books in December 2003

First edition published in the United Kingdom in February 2004

Translated and first published in South Korea in March 2004

All information is believed current and correct at time of writing. Some names have been omitted by request or changed to avoid embarrassment.

Unless denoted otherwise, all photographs are the work of the Mercury Books/ Daewoo Challenge team. The Front and Back Cover pictures were kindly supplied by GM Daewoo. In the event of any question arising as to the ownership of these or any other materials or illustrations, please contact Mercury Books, PO Box 3620, MK16 0XQ, England.

Editing: Brian Bollen; manuscript preparation: Angela Sherman and Sheila Plater.

ISBN: 0-9541432-3-X

Designed and typeset by Claire Hersant (E: clairehersant@mac.com)

Printed in England.

Which Way Next ?

- Story of the Daewoo Challenge

Comings and goings

Start/ Finish
Depart: (Luton) UK – Monday June 9
Arrive: (Pusan) Korea – Thursday October 2
Total: 115 days

Finishing parade
Incheon/ Seoul – Wednesday October 8

Countries visited (25) and capital cities (17)
UK, Holland, Belgium, France (Paris), Germany, Switzerland, Italy (Rome), Austria (Vienna), Hungary (Budapest), Serbia-Montenegro (Belgrade), Macedonia – the former Yugoslavia (Skopje), Greece (Athens), Turkey (Ankara), Georgia (Tbilisi), Azerbaijan (Baku), Kazakhstan, Uzbekistan (Tashkent), Afghanistan (Kabul), Pakistan, India (Delhi), Bangladesh (Dhaka), Thailand (Bangkok), Laos, Vietnam (Hanoi) and Korea (Seoul).

Distance driven
18,350 km

Total distance covered
Approx 24,000 km*

(*includes ferries from Greece to Turkey and across the Caspian Sea, by train from Kazakhstan into Uzbekistan, by plane from Termez to Kabul and from Dhaka to Bangkok, and by cargo vessel from Vietnam to South Korea)

Note: Also see "Nuts and Bolts" in Appendix 5

Which Way Next?

The original journey plan before SARS ruled out China
(for the final route map - see back cover)

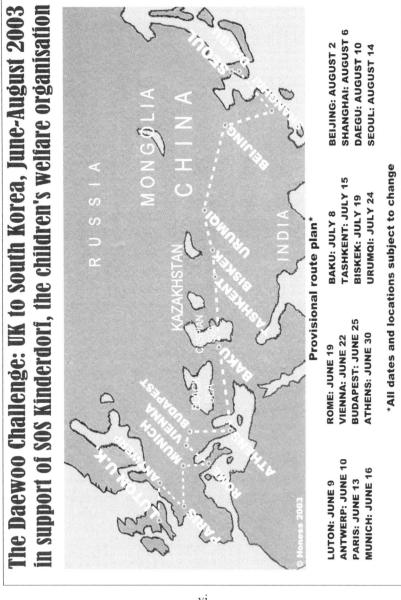

The Daewoo Challenge: UK to South Korea, June-August 2003
in support of SOS Kinderdorf, the children's welfare organisation

Provisional route plan*

LUTON: JUNE 9
ANTWERP: JUNE 10
PARIS: JUNE 13
MUNICH: JUNE 16

ROME: JUNE 19
VIENNA: JUNE 22
BUDAPEST: JUNE 25
ATHENS: JUNE 30

BAKU: JULY 8
TASHKENT: JULY 15
BISKEK: JULY 19
URUMQI: JULY 24

BEIJING: AUGUST 2
SHANGHAI: AUGUST 6
DAEGU: AUGUST 10
SEOUL: AUGUST 14

*All dates and locations subject to change

© Honess 2003

vi

CONTENTS

Appendices

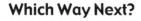

Which Way Next?
- Story of the Daewoo Challenge

*For Phil, my co-driver and courageous companion
and for children everywhere who have been deprived of a mother's love*

A great many people around the world helped to make the Daewoo Challenge a great success through their love, encouragement, help and kindness.

For those most closely involved with the project, special thanks must go to Phil McNerney, my partner in this great adventure, and to the Mercury Books team of Geoff Courtney, Angela Sherman, Tony Honess and Peter Hoare. Also, at GM Daewoo in Zurich, for their unceasing support and help, to the team of Hanspeter Ryser, Marc Kempe and Eric Neve; and at GM Daewoo Auto & Technology South Korea to Rob Leggat, Ken Hong and Rene Kreis. At the SOS Children's Villages headquarters in Innsbruck, the assistance and encouragement of Michaela Schalk and Helen Clarke was simply wonderful.

A mention, too, for Dr Kijoon Yu, head of the technical centre at GM Daewoo Auto & Technology in Bupyung, South Korea, who came up with the original concept of the Kalos car, and to Yves Fourdin from Ath in Belgium, for his great mechanical skills and knowledge. Without Dr Yu we wouldn't have had a car, and without M. Fourdin we wouldn't have completed the trip.

Along the way we received a fantastic amount of support, advice and hospitality from so many people – but for special services we awarded "caps" (GM Daewoo baseball variety). The following received them (or would have done if we had had enough!): Nina in Georgia, two small boys who got us into the Trabzon soccer stadium in Turkey, Christine Jafaar and Sandra (neé) Viroulet at GM Daewoo Paris who lent us their tights, the customs officer at Tbilisi who supports Arsenal FC, Agnes Roma at GM Daewoo Budapest, Ugur Zeynally at SOS Baku, (jointly) to Anwar Kholbaev of the UN, Col. Wolfgang Hoppe of the German Air Corps and Maj. Arthur Jongeneelen of 334 Sqn Eindhoven for their help in the airlift from Termez to Kabul, Satish Kumar of SOS in Delhi, Paula of SOS Italy, Lorella Zecchinelli of GM Daewoo Rome, Wasim at SOS Lahore, Yves de Cauwer at GM Daewoo Belgium, Kirsten Lattewitz of GM Daewoo Germany, Abu Sayeed Khan of Hellman's in Dhaka, Jung In Kim at Vidamco, Hanoi, John Kondominas of Daellas SA, Athens, and Denis Chick at GM Daewoo, Luton.

Many others, too numerous to mention, also gave us huge help and assistance. In particular, our thanks go to all management and staff at the following locations where the Challenge car made checkpoint or stopover visits:

SOS Children's Villages: Diessen (Germany), Rome (Italy), Imst (Austria), Budapest (Hungary), Athens (Greece), Baku (Azerbaijan), Tashkent (Uzbekistan), Lahore (Pakistan), Delhi & Calcutta (India), Dhaka (Bangladesh), Bangpoo (Thailand), Hanoi (Vietnam) and Daegu (Korea).

GM/GM Daewoo sites: Luton (UK offices), Breda on Dutch/Belgian border (European parts distribution centre), Paris (French HQ), Rome (Italian HQ), Vienna (new Nubira launch), Athens (Greek HQ), Tashkent (Uzbek. dealer), Delhi (Indian dealer), Bangkok (Thailand dealer), Hanoi (assembly plant, Vietnam), Seoul (world HQ, Korea).

viii

Which Way Next?

Introduction

WHEN the container vessel *Seven Seas Aurora* docked at the port of Pusan in South Korea just before midnight on Thursday October 2, she was five days behind schedule. Typhoon Maemi was the reason. Sailing out of the Gulf of Tonkin from the Vietnamese port of Haiphong, the 20,000-ton cargo ship had been forced to shelter for three days in the safety of Hong Kong's harbour as winds of 135mph lashed the region in one of the worst typhoons for almost a century.

Then she was held up for another 48 hours at Pusan, where the raging storm had wrought havoc to the dockside and forced a long line of ships to heave-to across the bay and await their turn to unload.

Inside one of the containers, safely strapped down to avoid any damage, was a small family hatchback car which had already survived several severe batterings on a four-month journey that had taken her halfway round the world.

Earlier that same day, on the other side of Pusan (Korea's second-largest city, known locally as Busan) eager motoring enthusiasts were hurrying in their thousands to the opening of an international motor show.

It was a big event in a nation where five of the world's major car-makers have helped to turn a previously faltering economy into one of the richest in Asia.

GM Daewoo Auto & Technology, investing heavily in the exhibition, has a magnificent stand featuring a range of gleaming cars, glamorous girl models and a hi-tech entertainment show, all aimed at putting their visitors firmly in a buying mood.

At the back of the display on a mural the size of a small house, is an elaborate map telling in words and pictures how one of their Kalos cars, driven by two British adventurers, has survived a marathon journey from England to Korea.

"Welcome to the Daewoo Challengers ..." says the legend at the top.

1

Which Way Next?

The car in front of it is a light blue Kalos, looking very smartly finished in glistening metallic paint. But keen-eyed visitors are quickly able to spot that it is not the same car they can see on the map, and that the adventuring drivers are particularly conspicuous by their absence. Their Challenge car is the one still cocooned in the hold of the *Seven Seas Aurora,* which is now waiting, five days late, in the line of ships anchored out in the bay.

Further north, 400km away on that same blue sky morning, a smartly dressed man with his head bowed low, is led into an office for questioning at the prosecutor's department of the Supreme Court in Seoul, the nation's capital, by Ahn Dae-Hee, chief of Korea's Central Investigation Bureau.

His name is Son Kil-Seung. He is the 61-year-old chairman of the SK Corporation, a conglomerate of telecommunications and oil refining companies, which has grown into the third-largest business in the country. He is also head of the Federation of Korean Industries, a lobby group for Korea's biggest corporations.

Within days he will admit to fraud and false accounting; accused of setting up a multi-million-dollar slush fund with his company's money to bribe the nation's top politicians for business favours.

Shortly afterwards, the Korean President Roh Moo-Hyun, facing calls for his impeachment, will threaten to dissolve the government.

The potential scandal is a sensational jolt to the nation.

But for many Koreans, the unfolding drama also bears disturbingly similar parallels to an earlier scandal, still fresh in their memories, which brought about the downfall of Kim Woo Choong, founder of the Daewoo Corporation and another industry icon.

Ahn Dae-Hee, the head of detectives, wants to ask Mr Choong what happened to an even bigger slush fund and two missing US$ billions in cash. But despite four years of trying, the nation's police chief and detective colleagues from forces around the world still can't track him down.

I tell you these things now because the events on that very same day in October weave together the strands of the most remarkable journey of

2

my lifetime – a journey which began on a whim and led to an adventure of excitement and danger that I shall never forget. It started in the town of Luton in the UK, a rather nondescript place not far north of London, and it ended in South Korea, the country that has worked an economic miracle for its 47 million people, bringing wealth and prosperity to a land which only 50 years ago was devastated by a war that left more than two million dead, wounded or missing, and a nation split in two.

With a friend, Phil McNerney, a young graduate with time on his hands after university, we took a car owned by GM Daewoo and drove it across 25 countries and 19,000km to raise money for SOS Children's Villages, the international child welfare organisation.

It took 115 days for the three of us to reach South Korea on our marathon journey. Our car, a Daewoo Kalos 1.4 with more than 8.000km already on the clock, was a family hatchback more usually suited to taking the kids to school or for popping along to the shops to buy some groceries.

Officially, our attempt was called the Daewoo Challenge, but we quickly nicknamed it "the longest shopping expedition in the world". We equally quickly christened our car the Greek Goddess after we discovered that Kalos is the Greek word for beautiful. She became such a part of our lives that we even finished up talking to her; at our most extreme moments, I swear she spoke back.

The journey was certainly a challenge. It was never meant to be a race or a rally; we had no support car or mobile back-up. The key objectives, as set out by GM Daewoo, our sponsors, were to make checkpoint visits to a number of locations in their transnational network, complete the journey to prove the capabilities of their Kalos car, and to achieve as much publicity as possible. My guess is that in the latter department especially they got the bargain of a lifetime.

For SOS Children's Villages, our charity partners – an organisation founded by the Austrian Hermann Gmeiner after World War II to provide secure homes and a mother's love for orphaned children – the objective was to publicise the charity's growth into a worldwide force, bringing hope - and a future - to more than 50,000 abandoned and destitute children in 131 countries. And, of course, to raise them some much-needed funds.

Which Way Next?

Children are an emotive cause. And children in need even more so. Their innocence in an often guilty world strikes at the hearts of everyone from the rich and famous to those who simply want to lend a hand. SOS Children's Villages, which now has a plan to expand its activities by 50% over the next five years, has many supporters.

To give some examples, they currently range from FIFA, the governing body of world soccer, to the family of Johnny Cash who, after his recent death, appealed for fans to send donations to SOS Children's Villages as a tribute to the singer's life, and to Michel van Velde and Elles Albering, a young Dutch couple who (as far as we know) are still on their own marathon journey from Holland to Beijing in an "old timer" VW campervan. We think we passed them somewhere on the road near Mount Olympus in Greece although, to be quite honest, we can't be really sure.

And now they have us, the family of GM Daewoo and Phil and me, whose combined efforts have put a not insignificant number of Euros of help the children's way.

When I approached GM Daewoo to sponsor the trip I did it with little more than hope. Phil and I don't know much about cars. He has got a degree in geology and is very handy with computers, and I make a living out of writing.

The idea came about because we both wanted to go teaching in China, but flying there seemed too easy and since Korea was nicely nearby, I simply asked GM Daewoo if they would lend us a car and we would do the rest. Remarkably for us, they said yes – and then neither of us could think of a good enough excuse to back down!

It all happened in quite a rush. For a variety of reasons there were only four months between my original approach and us setting off down the leafy lanes of Bedfordshire, England. Sometimes, if you have too long to think about things, you can finish up not doing them. In our case, if we had known what was going to happen, I'm not sure we would have gone at all.

We certainly hadn't done much homework – except to find out that General Motors, the world's largest car-making company, had not long before bought some of the assets of the bankrupt Daewoo car business in Korea and they might therefore be up for a bit of publicity.

Our hunch was right. But what we didn't know, until the very end, was why Daewoo had gone bust.

The remarkable story of Kim Woo Choong and his Daewoo corporation will presumably have no ending while he remains a fugitive. But, as far as I know, this is what happened:

In 1968, while the Koreans in the south of their divided country were finally making progress towards building a new economy, Mr Choong set up a small textile business with just US$10,000 and five employees.

His company grew with startling speed and in little more than 30 years he had built a giant conglomerate corporation (or *chaebol* as clustered corporate families are known locally) – the second-biggest in all of Korea – with businesses ranging from hotels to construction, ship-building, general trading and cars. They employed more than 18,000 staff in his country alone.

To many, he became a symbol of the nation's new spirit of enterprise and material gain. His personal wealth was large enough to put him well inside the *Fortune 500* world's richest individuals and the corporation he founded seemed highly profitable and a huge success.

The government, busy over-arching the "economic miracle" which would raise their country to 14th wealthiest in the league table of these things, honoured his business as a *chaebol* (the "chosen ones") along with three others, Hyundai, Samsung and Lucky Goldstar Electronics – family-run, giant corporations that were singled out for special support and favoured dealings in a strategy of "encouraging the fittest."

At that time, the four corporations were estimated to employ 500,000 people and effectively controlled the jobs of millions more through supplier companies and affiliates.

But something went horribly wrong.

Mr Choong, then 62 and a chain-smoking, colourful character, apparently left for a meeting in China one afternoon in September 1999 and never came back. Also missing, according to the investigating accountants, was US$2 billion dollars in cash. Furthermore, they discovered a gaping hole in the books down which a vast amount of company money had been siphoned into a special fund to pay off politicians for preferential decisions.

Choong's Daewoo car company, heavily over-borrowed and unable to pay its debts, was declared bankrupt, and the group as a whole subsequently collapsed.

Meanwhile, accusations of corruption, fraud and false accounting against Mr Choong and a large number of his senior executives – involving sums which surpass even the recent Enron and WorldCom scandals in the USA – remain unproven and on the file.

Four years later, and the police are still trying to find him. Korea's answer to Elvis, Lord Lucan and Shergar is rumoured to have been spotted in places as far apart as France and America, north and south. *Fortune* magazine managed to interview him somewhere in South-east Asia earlier this year, when, amongst many other things, he blamed the demise of his Daewoo car company on overambition. "I tried to do too much too fast," he is claimed to have said.

Another recently unconfirmed sighting was at the Hanoi Daewoo Hotel, a five-star luxury centre piece in the communist Vietnam capital, which was built with company cash and personally designed and furnished by his socialite wife Heeja Choong at an estimated cost of US$163 million in 1996.

Mrs Choong, who liked to be known as the "Lady of Seoul", was installed as chairwoman of the Daewoo Development Co., a subsidiary of the group, and opened seven hotels in Korea, China and Africa.

Cutting a stylish figure with a silver-topped ebony walking stick, she invited 3,000 guests including diplomats and politicians from across the world to the opening of the Hanoi Daewoo Hotel, which she lavishly decorated with fine art, porcelain, sculptures and marble.

In the grounds there is an 18-hole golf course and a swimming pool, which is thought to be the largest in Asia. Guests have included the Russian President Vladimir Putin and a host of senior political figures from China and the USA.

All of which kind of brings us back to Daewoo, the new GM Daewoo, and why they lent us a car.

Today, in Korea, GM Daewoo's new company, under an ambitious management team, has just finished its first year of operations and the ending of our epic journey virtually coincided with it.

Just as they would have wanted, our trip in their Kalos car – with all its twists and turns, changes of plan, excitement, danger and adventure, and all the publicity that those stories generated – has already drawn a great deal of media attention to the team now trying to restore the name and image of the Daewoo car brand.

We also hope it will have helped to build a better future for the children – now and yet to come – in the care of SOS Children's Villages.

This is the story of The Daewoo Challenge.

- Richard Meredith, South Korea, October 2003

Chapter 1
RED RAG TO A BULL

THE problem with still being an adventurer in your fifties is that no-one knows whether to take you seriously. "Hey, that's a good idea," says a pal when you spill out your latest scheme for a bit of hell-raising. But then they add: "I'll tell my son and see if he's up for it." Or, far worse, they hear you out then look you in the eye and say: "Wow – that would be quite something. But don't you think you're a bit old to do things like that!" I guess it's all part of life's conditioning.

And yet …and yet… The trouble with people like me is that if someone, anyone really, suggests that something can't be done, then a very swift and powerful reaction comes over me that says I want to prove them wrong. Just like waving a red rag at an old bull, you might say. It's in the genes, I suppose. Sometimes I look at my mother and think: "You were the one who made me this way!" And I can see it in her too; she's a lively lady, with an eventful past, and still setting out on her own adventures well into retirement.

As far as I can remember, the first time it occurred to me that a long – (and I mean *long*) – distance car drive could be a bit of an adventure, was on the road out from Miami along Florida's east coast. It wasn't just any old road. It was Highway One, America's original. I was on another adventure. I'd taken a year out to go back-packing, not as some fresh-faced teenager between college and university, but, yes, as an old codger in his fifties, who had had his fill of life's stresses and strains and needed a break from it all. I wrote a book about that too, a kind of Gap Year for Grown-ups I called it. But that, quite literally, is another story.

Let me digress for a moment. Back in Florida, on that other adventure, I was driving late one evening in a hire car, just meandering along, looking for somewhere to spend the night, when a sign reminded me I was on Highway One. If I'm honest it hadn't triggered much of my interest when I'd stopped at a café the day before to plan my route. But now it had - it had got that inquisitive gene inside me all worked up.

I got the big map book out in the motel bedroom and thumbed

through the pages following the road from north to south. All down the first page it went. And the second. And the third. Why, by the time I'd finished, I must have tracked it down a dozen pages and more. And that was the point. Highway One runs down the whole of the United States, from top to bottom. It becomes a tarmac'd artery up in Maine near the border with Canada and works itself all the way down the eastern seaboard to Key West at the very end of the island keys of Florida, more than 2,000 miles later.

These days it's been by-passed, under-passed and over-passed by dozens of freeways along much of its length as the towns and cities along it have grown and the traffic flows have escalated. But the old road still remains, out-of-date but not yet redundant, in urgent need of repair here and there and out-modishly narrow in places, but a national highway nonetheless.

Now heck, I'm thinking (with that so-adventurous mind of mine), what a magical journey it would be to travel down the whole long distance of Highway One, to make that journey along every yard of it, through every town of it, through every straight and narrow piece of it. Think of the millions, no zillions, of folk who must have driven along there over the years. Think of the history. Think of the changes it must have seen. Think of what's gone on: the daily dramas, the events, the incidents, the accidents - all of those happenings, past and present, witnessed by this ribbon of black and grey asphalt stretching away mile after mile across the horizons of the richest and most ambitious country on earth.

See what I mean? Why, I could stop in the towns, talk to the people, slip into the newspaper offices and the museums, dust off the old archives… find out what's been happening down this road of memories over all these years. Write a book about it? Quite a story! Just imagine.

Back in my home village in the pub one night, I had recounted the idea to Geoff, a writer friend of mine.

"See what I mean about my adventurous streak," I said. "Well, what do you think of that one?"

"M'm, just remember you're in your fifties now," said Geoff. Typical.

Which Way Next?

"It's not a bad idea, I'll give you that, but surely you can't be serious about wandering off for months at a time on some kind of half-baked whim? Why don't you leave it to someone much younger - or wait until you retire and have nothing better to do!" Typical again.

So we drank our beer and went on to discuss the world, the universe and everything a dozen more times.

When I think about it now, as a writer, I guess that although I knew I had come up with a good storyline for a book – maybe "The Life and Times of Highway One" or something like that – I had rapidly discounted it with the thought that surely someone would have done it already.

Ah, but what neither of us knew that night, was that within a little over six months, I would indeed be setting out on a marathon driving journey – not down the highways and byways of America, but from the UK right across Europe, Central Asia, the Indian subcontinent and then to South Korea which, let's be honest, no average man in the average Western street had known much about until the soccer authorities decided it should co-host the last World Cup.

Superlatives are dangerous words, but I doubted that very few would have made the journey before, fewer still would have written a book about it – and none at all would have done it in a Daewoo.

What's true too is that for me, until now, my understanding of a long drive was either something which led to the homes of the rich and famous, or a feat of sporting prowess that people boasted about on the golf course.

Anyway, the reason for that comes later and this is for now. So I'll start by explaining why Geoff and I had met up in the pub that night.

Years ago, probably when most people would think I was actually the right age for going on adventures like this one, I had a job working as a reporter on a newspaper in Hertfordshire. It was an evening paper, which brought the news nightly to thousands of families in a bustling town in the northern Home Counties where the lower price of homes, just beyond the outer fringes of London, was a major attraction. Like many evening papers, the *Echo* was eventually unable to compete with the instant news delivery of TV and radio and its circulation dwindled to the point where, with its neighbouring twin the *Post*, both were shut down.

But in my time there, the newsroom was always buzzing with the action and activity of a newspaper office with several deadlines daily – and sometimes hourly. We had a good team. The stresses of working under pressure often bring out the best in people; they brought us together, created friendships and *camaraderie*, a great team spirit and, as in all situations like that, they soon showed up those with talent and those without.

Geoff was a bit of a hero in the office. He was the motoring correspondent for both our papers with a regular weekly column of his own and a clutch of motoring businesses on the patch to write about every day: Vauxhall, then one of the UK's biggest car manufacturers, was on the doorstep at Luton; trucks were manufactured over at Bedford; glamorous hand-made Aston Martins (made famous through the James Bond films and a variety of celebrity owners like the Prince of Wales) purred out of the factory at nearby Newport Pagnell; and topping the lot was Silverstone with its Grand Prix race circuit and entourage of celebrities half a dozen stops up the motorway.

Being the motoring correspondent was a "plum" job and for someone so in love with cars as Geoff, it must have seemed close to heaven. But for people like me, the ones who know no more about cars than where to put the key to start them in the morning, reading about them in the paper had no greater priority than ads for second-hand socks.

Or at least it wouldn't have had if it hadn't been for Geoff. His column was so interesting and witty that even for car novices like me it was always worth reading.

There's an argument that motoring columns have become a devalued lot. Maybe it's the need for commercial survival experienced by so many newspapers these days, maybe it's simply that hardly any papers employ writers with enough knowledge on the subject. Whatever. The fact is that most so-called motoring columns consist of two or three hundred scrappy words written around a car that was "kindly lent to our motoring writer by company X, a local garage, to road test this week." Frequently, too, there's an advert from that same garage placed handily alongside. In a harsh world for the independently-minded Editor, newspaper managers see it as a convenient way of attracting extra advertising revenue, garage proprietors delight because only nice things are said about their latest models, and journalists get to have the thrill of parking some gleaming, super-wotsit Mark 6 outside their girlfriend's house and kicking the wheels as if they own it.

But Geoff and his column were never like that and we loved him for it; or maybe we admired him for it. Good journalists are a hard-bitten lot. They have to be. Or should be, shall we say. It takes a certain cynicism to sort out fact from fiction, a depth of knowledge to argue your corner, a freedom of mind not to be swayed by profit margins and expense-account lunches. And to us reporter-types, Geoff seemed to have all of that. His column was instantly lively, often irreverent and always readable. He told it like he found it, and if he didn't like the whatever-car-it-was, he said so – dents and all.

As time went by, I left the paper to go and do other things, but even before our night in the pub talking about America's Highway One, Geoff's path and mine had crossed several times. When the *Post-Echo* closed he had taken a job with his beloved Aston Martin company and joined their public relations department. "A bit like going over the wall," he called it. "But with a cushion on the other side."

Evidently he was good at it too, earning himself the accolade of head of Aston Martin's worldwide PR and helping them to enhance the international reputation of their cars.

He came to be the receiver of journalists' calls and not the maker of them. Aston Martin is such a magnetic name in the motor industry, every newspaper or magazine columnist would give their right elbow to be loaned one for an hour, never mind a week, for a bit of freebie road testing. Geoff's network of contacts grew and grew. If there was anyone worth talking to for their knowledge of cars, where to drive them and how to publicise the trip, it was Geoff. And I knew it.

As it turned out, Geoff the Mediaman was my first recruit in this hair-brained scheme to drive a car to South Korea.

Chapter 2
NOTHING VENTURED, NOTHING GAINED

WELL OK, so Geoff's thoughts about me and Highway One didn't exactly get off the ground in the pub that night, but they certainly set me thinking.

As a journalist, and especially as a reporter, time frames are about as short as a Kylie Minogue skirt. "There's been a plane crash down at Heathrow, Meredith; get down there and cover it," commands the Editor. Or "Politician X is making a speech tonight about saving the whales in Addis Ababa. See what he has to say will you?" Write up the story, get it in the paper then move on to the next one. Sometimes there's a follow-up, but often not. The story is done and dusted, yesterday's news is history and all that. But being a writer is different. A book is a major event. The story needs stamina and substance and, to be frank, it can be hard work to conjure up a storyline with enough material to keep a reader intrigued for a couple of hundred pages or more.

I like to write about travel. It's been a passion of mine for as long as I can remember. It's there in the genes again I guess. My mother has been able to travel for most of her life and has been to places I didn't know existed; my brother flies planes for a living, one week he's in America, the next India, and he loves it too. Then there's the other side of me, which craves adventure. Put the two together and it's a devil of a combination.

My first book was a great adventure and if ever I needed convincing that travelling and writing about it was what I really wanted to do, then here was the proof. Wandering around the world falling into adventures (and misadventures) was a great storyline. But what should I write about next?

I had juggled with ideas for months, chatted them through with friends, pored over maps, read other people's stuff, watched never-ending TV looking for anything with a foreign flavour, scanned the newspapers, flicked through the mags.

Which Way Next?

In the end, I had settled for a trip to China as the source for my next book and I had planned to undertake a teaching contract while I was there to give me a base for my travels.

China seemed to have everything for a writer like me. Here was a nation, the most populated in the world, which is, right now, undergoing the most profound changes in its history. Like pre-World Cup South Korea, it's still a land of great mystery to most Westerners; a land of intrigue, of political struggle, of poverty and new-found wealth; a country of huge mountains, vast plains, empty deserts, and long-running rivers … oh yes, and of no little danger either.

Here was travel, adventure and certainly enough news to satisfy the die-hard reporter in me. So that was that; decision made. I would travel to China and stay there for six months at least. The publishers said they were happy I had chosen the "right kind of place for my kind of book". It was all the reassurance I needed. There was no knowing what would happen to me there, let alone whether my stories would be good enough to fill a book they could sell in large quantities later, but they would be glad to receive a manuscript from me after I got back.

I could not have foreseen the events that would soon turn the whole trip on its head and lead me into an even more exciting adventure.

But like I said, the decision had been made. So I began to get the planning under way: visas to apply for, airlines to contact, medicals to arrange, house to let, things to buy, business affairs to put in order ...

And that's how it was – until my meeting that night with Geoff the Mediaman.

It usually leads to trouble when people say I shouldn't do something. Remember? Geoff didn't think much of my plan for driving all the way down America, he said. Get the idea? OK then, how about driving to China?

I toyed with the notion for all of two seconds. Well why the heck not!

These days, when I don't know enough about something then - like most of us, I guess - I turn to the Internet for answers. The screen scrolled into action. Travel to China? Roads? Directions? Distances? I clicked the questions into the search engine.

And now cars. Fast ones? Reliable ones? Comfortable ones? Cars you wouldn't be seen dead in? Cars you would be seen dead in? "Excuse me," I asked the Internet gently, "what car do you suggest I drive to China?" Strangely enough, for a globe-girdling network that appeared to know everything, it now seemed to know nothing. But I was about to find out anyway.

I discovered the name of Hanspeter Ryser on the end of a press release about GM Daewoo's plans to launch a new range of cars. He was Director of Public Affairs in Europe, it said, and he invited anyone who wanted to know more to contact him for further information.

So I did.

His name hadn't turned up in my first session in front of the computer looking for answers in my travel-to-China puzzle. Nor the next. I had sat there for hours dodging from site to site and from image to image, until my eyes were weary and my brain be-fuddled. Scraps of paper riddled with scribbled information lay scattered all around the desk.

Finally there it was: the press release signed by M. Ryser (in Switzerland of all places) which spoke loudly from the screen to me saying: "Hey, read every word of this Meredith, because it's like I wrote it just for you!"

There were three (at least) good reasons why the information in front of me had my open-mouthed attention:

- Firstly, the manufacturers of Daewoo cars were based in South Korea and were therefore just a flea-hop, by comparison to virtually anywhere else, from China;
- secondly, Daewoo (the marque) had been bought only the year before by General Motors who, as the largest conglomerate of car-makers in the world, could most certainly afford to lend me a car; and
- thirdly, Daewoo (the cars) would shortly be launching a new range of vehicles and could therefore do with some helpful publicity.

Perfect! I cleared the pile of paper scraps from around the phone and dialled the Swiss number.

"M. Ryser, Hanspeter Ryser? Is that you?" I ventured.

"Yes," came the answer in very good English.

15

Which Way Next?

"This is Richard Meredith calling from the UK."

"Yes?" There was a question in the answer. I felt a sudden dryness in my mouth.

"Hanspeter, you don't know me and I don't know you, but I was just wondering if you could let me have one of your cars to do a test drive."

"Oh?" There is another question in the answer. And then, after a pause, "And where exactly did you have in mind?"

"Well, I actually have an idea to drive one of your cars from the UK to South Korea."

Ah, now that's torn it, I'm thinking. There is another pause, longer this time.

"Oh, I see! Well that's quite an idea," said M. Ryser with the kind of semi-mockery that usually comes more easily from the British than the Swiss.

And so my story starts. Ten minutes later and Hanspeter has heard me out. Author ... China ... Daewoo ... General Motors ... South Korea ... new range ... publicity ... I string it all together with hardly a pause for breath.

"Are you still there?" I inquire.

"Yes, I'm still listening," he says and then: "It's certainly a crazy idea."

Oh, then that's the end of that, I'm thinking. Yet there had been something in his voice; something positive.

"Yes, look I know it's crazy, but isn't it sometimes the craziest ideas that make all the difference?"

He comes back: "Very well, I'm not saying we would be interested, but neither am I saying it's out of the question. I will want to think about it. Put your proposal down in an email and send it to me, will you?" I said I would, scarcely suppressing my delight.

And then I thought to add something right off the cuff.

"Isn't life strange?" I said. "I bet you never imagined that someone would just ring you up in the middle of one afternoon and ask you to lend him a car to drive halfway round the world."

"Er, no," said Hanspeter, "no-one has ever done that to me before. But we always try, as an organisation, to be open to ideas, even crazy ones. So let me have your plans."

And I think I knew then, even as I put the phone back on the hook, that I had stumbled on a very good way to get to China.

Some things, they say, are meant to be. And others not. Right now, I supposed, this one might go either way. But at least Hanspeter had not laughed me off the court and there had been enough in his conversation to give me some encouragement.

Within 48 hours, when I sent my message back to him, I was also able to put in it that I already had the first member of my team.

"Geoff Courtney, well-connected motoring journalist and former head of worldwide public relations at Aston Martin, will be able to handle all the publicity for the trip," I wrote.

"You did what?" said Mediaman with total incredulity when I told him the story. But he soon came around.

"Yes, you can say I'll do the publicity if it will help. But no-one will believe it – no-one would be mad enough to drive to Chingford in a Daewoo, let alone to China!"

"Well I would," I told him, "and do you know why? ... It's because you said I couldn't."

Chapter 3
CRAZY ENGLISHMAN

I REMEMBER once being with my father, who had a lifetime's love affair with Citroens, driving along a busy suburban road in North London when one of the front wheels suddenly decided to leave the rest of the car and headed towards a queue waiting for a bus on the other side.

By some minor miracle they all managed to dive out of the way in the nick of time and the wheel continued harmlessly rolling along on its solo journey into someone's front garden.

We later discovered that a forgetful mechanic was to blame. He had failed to tighten a wheel bolt during the car's service that morning, but thanks to the Citroen's 'floating' suspension system, which lifted the wheel-less axle off the road in an instant, both we, the car and the startled passengers of the No 107 to Finchley Central, escaped without a scratch.

Then there was another time, again with my father, when a car crashed into ours down a narrow country lane. The other driver, who claimed it was totally my father's fault, was found guilty in court of driving carelessly and had his licence taken away. But for me, the whole affair, and especially the trauma of standing in the witness box being cross-examined by an aggressive and high-powered lawyer, left a lasting impression that, quite frankly, cars were something I could do without.

On the other hand (those genes again) maybe the auto-amnesia comes from my mother's side, for she still thinks a dipstick is a term of abuse, needs to ask a man (oh, God forbid) to change a tyre, and invokes an all-embracing answer to any serious-sounding noises coming from the engine by turning up the radio to drown them out.

At any rate, while most of the friends I grew up with spent their time talking about cars, sport and girls (the order progressively reversed as we grew older) I found their conversations about horse power, engine capacity, transmissions and the like, about as interesting as the love-life of a snail.

That isn't to say I haven't driven cars, of course. In fact I think I have owned one of some type or another since the age of 18, when I passed my test at the second attempt.

My first try, taken in a girlfriend's car, ended in disaster when the shopping we had collected on the way to the test centre shot off the back seat as I over-reacted to the emergency stop procedure. The examiner and I then spent 20 minutes clearing up the splodge of broken eggs, squashed tomatoes, crushed biscuits and the contents of a jar of honey whose lid had parted company from its contents.

Still, at least he saw the funny side. "I'm afraid you made a mess of that," he said, handing me a failure notice and heading off to the washroom to clean himself up.

My first car was a disaster, too. It was an old Ford Anglia with a go-faster engine transplanted into it from something else, which the bloke in the pub guaranteed me would out-race anything from the traffic lights. Soon after I bought it, I was powering up the gentle slope along the street where I lived when something under the bonnet let out a noise like a large bazooka and the car rolled powerlessly into the gutter in a haze of blue smoke. None of my car-mad mates could get it going again, and neither could I find the bloke in the pub to ask for my £35 back.

I have certainly always had a driving licence and never had more than a few points on it for minor offences like being caught on camera for speeding. Over the years I must have driven hundreds of thousands of miles - but never anything like the trip I was now proposing to South Korea.

In fact, thinking back, the furthest I can ever remember travelling on a single-journey car trip was with Ian, another of those friends from the early days, who was the proud possessor of a TVR.

What a powerful beast it was; bright green, fast as an arrow, and an eye-turner wherever it went.

Strange how the personalities of cars are often the totally opposite to those of their owners. Or, at least, they seem to be. Ian was a diminutive, shy kind of bloke who did something with computers, but this car of his was all have-a-go hero and testosterone sleek.

He took me down to the South of France in it – we went from home to beach in less than 24 hours including stops for beers, but the under-carriage insisted on arguing with some of those rural French roads and

Which Way Next?

by the time we got down to St Tropez (well where else does anyone go with a car like that?) most of his exhaust system had decided it was safer to let go of the rest. The resulting roar caught the ear of every *gendarme* – and every good-looking girl – on the Cote d'Azur, but it cost us a small fortune in welding fees before we could drive it home.

Talking of sports cars, or racing cars even, my cousin Anthony needs to step forward here. I had thought of him even before I rang Hanspeter in Switzerland that day, because I knew that if ever I got involved in something to do with cars then Tony would want to fit in the picture.

Anthony has had an extraordinary life. He was brought up in a not-very-big suburban house that was always full of children. His mother had four of her own, plus a succession of others she wanted to foster. Poor Tony – often he would find that a bed on the floor was all he came home to if he went out for the evening. He used to spend a lot of time visiting us and I'm not surprised. He must have been looking to escape from it all.

Anyway, Tony was another who loved cars with a passion. And not just any old cars. He liked racing cars as a hobby and a sport.

For years he would hang about the pits at Brands Hatch, not far from his home in Brighton, watching the drivers hurtling round at breakneck speed, snorting the whiff of high octane fuel, and catching himself a piece of the action. Then he got involved in the nuts and bolts of the thing, literally, joining one of the engine preparation teams for cars in Formula 1 and Formula Ford (including the Penske-Tyrell team of Danny Sullivan, a former winner of the Indianapolis 500).

To everyone's amazement he sometimes got into the driver's seat of those beasts himself - amazing because he is actually without a left hand, being born with only bobbles of skin (later removed) in place of fingers in one of those reminders of nature that we can't always have everything we want.

Yet did he let such a minor difficulty become a handicap? Did he heck! I would back my cousin Tony in any car-driving contest against the next man – one-handed or not.

Once, I remember him driving me in the country lanes near Hitchin in Hertfordshire. We were just about to enter a big right-hand bend doing a speed that was distinctly faster than average, when the nearside front tyre blew out. Bang! Just like that.

So what did he do? Calm as a Schumacher he just nudged down the gears with the stump of his left hand while his muscular right arm fought the steering wheel to keep us not just on the road, but on our side of it, while a large fuel tanker hurtling towards us from the opposite direction passed safely by.

I think it took me fully five minutes to say anything at all, by which time Tony had already jacked up the car and put on the spare.

These days, being a little later on in life, his only pilgrimages are to Silverstone for the British Grand Prix and to Monaco. He's a bit more sedate in his driving, but he's turned into a wizard with a camera, shooting top-quality action pictures (often at race meetings) for agency and magazine editors and passing on his knowledge by giving lectures to amateur enthusiasts.

A driver/mechanic and an excellent photographer, Tony would make a wonderful addition to the team.

"Hey Tony, what do you think of my latest idea?" I call him down in Brighton.

He listens to the story. "A Daewoo?" he says at length with a query in his voice. "Are you sure they've got one that will get you that far?"

And then there's a chuckle "Yes, of course they must have! And yes, of course you can count me in. I'll have trouble getting away from the camera shop for more than a couple of weeks, but that should be enough to get you on your way. Tell them I'm in on it, then let me know if there's anything I can do to help with planning. South Korea you say? That's the other side of China, isn't it? My goodness, there will be a huge amount to get organised."

"I know," I said – but I put down the phone with a smile on my face several miles wide.

Something inside me is beginning to hum: *Que sera sera,* whatever will be, will be … Some things are meant to happen, remember? And I am getting the distinct feeling that this is one of them.

So, with my favourite photographer now on the team, that makes three of us so far: myself, Mediaman and Snapper.

Next day I email Hanspeter with my first proposal including the project title: The "Daewoo Challenge" and spelling out our concept of driving one of their cars to South Korea, not as a race or a rally, but with the purpose of gaining them as much publicity and promotion as possible in exchange for their sponsorship of the trip. The purpose for our team, I point out, will be to take part in a modern story of travel and adventure - and I attach Geoff's and Tony's impressive-looking CVs.

Thanks to the Internet, I have done my homework. The setting-off date I put forward is the beginning of June. That's less than four months away, but it fits in with the press announcement for launching GM Daewoo's new range.

I have also had my China teaching contract through which specifies that I must start there on September 1.

So that's it then, start the drive from the UK at the beginning of June, finish in South Korea three months later, then fly on to China. There will be so much to do and not much time to do it. But at least I now have the outline of a plan.

"OK, let's see what you make of this crazy idea," I mutter to myself as I press the button and send my email off to Switzerland.

I visualise Hanspeter, who as yet I have not even met, reading it on his screen over there in Zurich.

"My goodness," I can hear him say, "that mad Englishman was serious about this idea after all!"

Chapter 4
STOKING THE MEDIA FIRE

I AM having one of those days when I ask myself a lot of questions. Whether it's in the written press, TV or radio, the only way to guarantee publicity is to pay for it with advertising. It costs a fortune and I should know – I have been around the media industry most of my life – and so has Geoff, who will mastermind the publicity efforts for our team. And so has Hanspeter and his GM Daewoo team in Switzerland.

I imagine them now, having a huddle over my email proposal. The key questions they will be asking themselves are: How much will it cost to provide a car and sponsorship for Meredith and Company to drive this journey? And how much free media publicity are we likely to get?

Because there is no guarantee of unpaid publicity it becomes a matter of judgment and, at the bottom line, I know their decision will come down to a purely commercial decision, no matter how much they may like the idea, or even me and my enthusiastic bunch of people.

They will also be questioning whether the type of publicity will be good for the corporate 'image' it gives to readers about the quality of Daewoo cars, their economy, reliability, comfort and ... well ... their staying power. In short, will their company sell more cars as a result of our trip?

Yes, that's the long and short of it – these will be the big questions on which our project will either attract GM Daewoo's sponsorship, or not.

I visualise myself as the news editor on a publication – any publication, somewhere, anywhere, along our route with a newly arrived story on my desk about this strange affair of an ageing Englishman driving halfway across the world simply to prove, he says, that "You Can Do It In A Daewoo". There will be a thousand things competing for coverage in their publication that day. But will they put this on the schedule – or in the bin?

I weigh up the pros and cons. Yes, I decide, I'm pretty sure they would run it – and I consider some of the reasons why:

Which Way Next?

. . . .

News values are a moveable feast. What interests readers today may just as easily not interest them tomorrow. In the UK newspaper business, outside the specialist pages like sport and finance, only royalty, babies and pets are exempted from this rule because they always get top priority. But 'firsts' of anything usually get an extra rating too.

Is it a 'first' for anyone to drive from the UK to South Korea? This will be an important angle in publicity for us. Certainly none of the people so far involved with the project has ever heard of it being done, but superlatives, as always, are dangerous words. I decide to check it out, as best I can, with my friend the Internet.

Ah, now here's a thing: Europe to China has been done already, I discover. Very rarely, but a completed journey nonetheless. It happened first in 1907 and it's quite a story.

With the motor industry hardly into first gear, but already arousing an atmosphere of excitement and competition, the motoring correspondent of the French newspaper *Le Matin* asked: "Will anyone agree to go, this summer, from Peking to Paris by automobile?"

According to the reports I've seen, five drivers stepped forward to take up the challenge and after many months of planning, began a 10,000-mile journey which featured in newspaper stories around the world and captured enormous public attention. In what was in effect the first-ever international motor rally, four cars completed the adventure from Peking (or Beijing as it is now known) to Paris with hardly a map worthy of the name and along roads that in places would pass as no more than cart tracks today.

The first car home was driven by the Italian Prince Scipione Borghese accompanied by *Le Matin's* correspondent (or a man from the *Daily Telegraph* if you believe another account) and the Prince's chauffeur who, on this occasion, left most of the driving to his master and acted as mechanic instead.

The trip took them just 62 days in an open-topped Itala with a 7.4 litre engine, no front brakes and a top speed of 60 mph. It finished three full weeks ahead of the others - two 10hp de Dion-Boutons from France and a lightweight 25hp Spyker from Holland. The fifth car, a tiny French Contal tri-cycle, hopelessly under-powered, valiantly gave up the chase.

The reporter from *Le Matin* wrote a book about the race, which later appeared in 13 languages and remained on the best-seller lists in Italy for the next 30 years. I haven't read all of it, but an extract tells me their biggest problems were getting stuck in mud and excessive hospitality. Rumour also has it there were some minor difficulties with marauding nomads and bomb-throwing Bolsheviks in Russia.

Ominously, my research also tells me that in 1997, when there was a re-enactment of the race, it took the organisers 18 months just to struggle through all the bureaucratic and political restrictions of our modern world.

Anyway, so far so good then. No-one, as far as I could tell, had ever attempted to drive a route from the UK to South Korea (or, to be more precise, from Luton – home of GM Daewoo in the UK – to Seoul, home of the car's manufacturing base).

It would indeed be a motoring 'first', providing a story of interest, not just for motoring enthusiasts everywhere, but for a much wider readership. My research had passed the first test: there really did seem every chance that the trip could achieve our would-be sponsor's Number One objective: a great deal of publicity!

But next, and no doubt a little disconcertingly for Daewoo, I had to think through the question of corporate image.

Now, innocent as I might be about all things mechanical, I can't say it had escaped my notice that whenever I mentioned the name of GM Daewoo, especially in motoring circles, people had a tendency to fall about laughing.

"Drive to Korea in a Daewoo? You must be joking!" was the most usual response.

"A Daewoo? You'll only get there if there's a following wind," was another.

In other words, let's just say it had already become pretty clear to me that Daewoo might have a credibility problem.

The advertising industry calls it building a brand image. Business gurus, and those who study these things, talk about corporate cultures and product positioning. But whatever they call it, the fact remains that consumers, over time, come to have a perception about particular products. They may rate them as good-for-value, or good-for-quality, reliability, consistency or the like, but products get themselves a reputation – for better or worse.

In the motor industry Mercedes and BMW are perceived as high quality, Volkswagens are good for reliability and Daewoos are ...well ... (at least in the UK) not thought to be good for much at all.

Mediaman has been putting me in the picture.

Motoring's butt of bar-room jokes used to be Ladas, he tells me. "They are renowned for (amongst the more polite things) their ability to go backwards faster than they go forward. Reliant Robins are reliable only for "robin'" their owners of something or other. And Skodas ..." His voice trails off in contempt.

Rightly or wrongly these perceptions have become established in the marketplace and it takes a long time, and a shedload of marketing money, to re-build an image even when huge programmes of product improvement, services or price correction have been achieved.

Which is where we come to Daewoo.

The Company has had its problems, my research on the Internet has told me that. It was owned until 2002 by the enormous South Korean trading conglomerate Daewoo International Corporation, until its essentially bankrupt car-making division, together with much of its worldwide sales operation, was taken under the wing of the even bigger General Motors Corporation of America in a deal that saved thousands of jobs for the factories in Seoul.

General Motors, whose stable already includes big-name car brands like Cadillac, Chevrolet, Buick, Vauxhall, Opel and Saab, is the largest car manufacturer in the world with 17% of the total global market. According to the website, they are investing zillions of dollars in Daewoo, launching new vehicles, improving the range, and generally re-building the much-battered reputation of their latest family member.

So here's the publicity thought: it seems that no-one will expect a Daewoo to get even halfway to South Korea. But Mediaman, Snapper and I can prove them all wrong - and give the world's biggest carmaker a hand with its image-building efforts at the same time.

Remember waving the red rag to an old bull? Now this is what I call a real Challenge!

And then there is the small matter of world events.

When Prince Scipione Borghese was doing his thing, reports spoke of the trouble he had from marauding nomads and bomb-tossing Bolsheviks. That may have been nearly 100 years ago but has anything really changed much?

Danger and excitement attract publicity – and as we start to plan our journey, today's world seems hell-bent on throwing up as many problems as ever.

Researching the northerly route taken by those stalwarts in 1907 tells me they had major problems crossing the Ural Mountains and the Russian Steppes. Believe it or not, things aren't much better now, I learn, with unmade roads, frequent mudslides and yes, marauding bandits.

So the Russian route looks a non-starter. Or at least it is for now.

Then there's the southerly route followed by contestants in the anniversary race of 1997. They went through Afghanistan, where a number of people are still anxious to have a word with the elusive arch-terrorist Osama bin Laden after recent historic events.

Not so good there either then. What about Iraq?

It's March 20, 2003, a Thursday. Mediaman and I have just spent all afternoon with GM Daewoo's top PR man in the UK. For the last few days, American and British troops have been rumbling ominously forward towards Iraq. And today – boom! US President George W. Bush announces that war has officially started.

"Not a good time to get caught between Iraq and a hard place then," I joke to the Daewoo man.

Already, our proposed route has changed more often than a supermodel on a fashion shoot. And now that war has broken out we change it again – up across the northern part of Turkey and as far from its lower border with Iraq as we can get.

And then there's China.

Now the short version of this particularly long story is that a disease called Severe Acute Respiratory Syndrome (SARS) is turning out to have been on the loose in China for several months. They knew it apparently, but for quite a long time they forgot to tell anyone.

Unfortunately it kills people, somewhere between 100 and 200 so far, or puts them in hospital, over 3,000 worldwide to date, and that's apparently just the beginning. It is a previously unknown virus with no antidote and according to latest reports the outbreak is expected to spread rapidly.

Which Way Next?

So it's obviously not such a good idea to be planning a car journey through China right now.

And I haven't even touched on the situation in North Korea, the South's militant neighbour which my over-worked Internet tells me daily has closed its border, is re-activating its nuclear bomb capability and is threatening to pour hell, fire and damnation over its "sworn enemy" America.

Mmmmm...obviously not so promising there either.

Danger, excitement, wars, plagues, fear of the unexpected ... this trip was already looking like having all the makings of an amazing adventure. And we hadn't even set off yet.

I could feel another email to Hanspeter coming on.

"You want publicity? If our little expedition doesn't produce enough news material to fill a library, I'll bet you that Switzerland wins the next World Cup, the Rugby World Cup," I am tempted to write - although I put it a little more diplomatically than that.

Chapter 5
TEAM TALK

ZURICH is instantly what any visitor would expect from a city in Switzerland. I had been there before during a brief stopover to somewhere else. It was only for 24 hours, but that was enough time for me to wander through some of the old quarter with its narrow alleys and ancient churches, and to see the city blocks of faceless offices and to stroll down the elegant Bahnhofstrasse with its glittering array of shops and superstores on my way from the station to the lake. It's a sophisticated place where buildings of well-preserved history attempt to blend with their modern-day cousins of concrete and glass and where the prosperous citizens hurry about their daily business along orderly and well-sanitised streets.

A metro-gnomic city, I think to myself.

And now I have gone there again at the request of Hanspeter and his colleagues. I think my last email must have done it. They wanted to meet this whoever-you-are-of-an-Englishman with the crazy idea. Well, that and the prospect of a great deal of publicity, I supposed.

The relationship had been going well. Hanspeter had recently been passing me onto his colleague Eric, the quietly spoken manager of product communications, for more telephone conversations. There had been several. We had begun to develop the plan, made promises about being open and trustworthy, set a number of key objectives. "Let's begin with the thought of this being a possible partnership where everyone gets something they want and no-one feels they are out of balance," Eric had said. It was all very positive.

But relationships on the telephone are never good enough. "Now we need to meet you," he said.

He collected me from the airport, a rather boyish figure with sports jacket and neat trousers. The voice was the same - soft and unhurried - and his hand came up only hesitantly in a wave. His shyness quite surprised me. We drove the short distance to Glattbrugg on the fringe of the city where General Motors (and now Daewoo) have their European headquarters.

"Here is Hanspeter," said Eric, introducing me gently to his director as I came through the door into their nicely carpeted suite.

I clasped his hand. "Remember the madman with the crazy plan?" There is a twinkle in his eye and he takes his time to look me up and down.

I had dithered at home about what to wear. For someone wanting to set out on a drive across some of the…shall we say…less comfortable parts of the world, a suit and tie had not seemed very appropriate. But this was a kind of business trip after all, so jeans and a T-shirt hadn't seemed right either.

In the end I had decided on casual trousers, a bomber-style jacket and a colourful rugby shirt, emblazoned, as they mostly are these days, with the name of an international company with a well-known product. I was, let's face it, wanting to be sponsored myself.

As with Eric, it was strange to put another face to the voice I had spoken to by phone and emailed.

Hanspeter was about my own age, I should think. Immediately he gave out a business-like aura of knowledge and experience, but there was something else. Yes, that was it: an air of approachableness and a mind that was receptive to ideas. I could just feel it.

I noticed him look at the name on my shirt. Then he smiled. "Well, let's see if we can do something with this plan of yours," he said.

And that was the way it all began.

We were soon joined by another colleague, Marc, a younger man who was brought up in Essex and now counts himself a Europhile with an excellent command of English, French and German. He, I understand, will be our main point of contact. Thankfully, since my grasp of foreign languages is not so good, we are able to conduct the whole meeting in English.

We talk about the car. Have they got anything in their range that will get me halfway across the world?

They take me through the list. A new range of cars is to be launched across Europe as part of GM's investment into the Korean company they tell me.

"These are exciting times for GM Daewoo," says Eric, and he begins to go into comprehensive detail about cubic capacity, engine mountings, braking systems and the like.

I think I get the drift; but my eyes are soon glazing over at the technicalities of it all.

In the end they settled on providing a Kalos[1] for me. A Kalos, they said, was one of their best-sellers. It, too, was being re-designed and improved in a whole variety of ways (excuse me if I can't remember all the details). It would have to be specially modified for the trip but it was versatile, had enough space inside for me, a co-driver and all our kit, a strong engine and – most important of the lot, it seemed to me – they were sure it would get us there.

We went downstairs to their underground car park for a brief look at one.

And what, I asked Marc, excusing my ignorance of all the technical stuff that had gone before, does Kalos mean?

"It's the Greek word for beautiful," he said.

She looked rather small. And not exactly beautiful to me!

"Oh, well that's all right then," I said.

I am pleased and relieved that the meeting is going so well. The attitude of this trio of GM Daewoo's top people in Zurich has been so positive and encouraging that already I feel able to discuss which route we should take.

I had also come with the thought that maybe we should link the Challenge to some worthwhile charity or other (I actually had UNICEF in mind) for some serious fund-raising. And this, too, was quickly solved.

---

[1] Footnote for the technically minded: GM Dawoo's original Kalos has a 1.4 litre engine with 61 KW/83 hp.

Two new versions have been launched to extend the range-a smaller 1.2 litre engine with 53 KW/72hp, and the larger 1.4 litre 16 valve unit with 69kW/94 hp combined with an automatic transmission. A five-door hatchback was launched in 2002 and a four-door hatchback variant with a separate luggage compartment became available in some markets in 2003. The shape and form for the cars was created by Giorgetto Guigiaro at Ital design.

Modifications for the Daewoo Challenge car included: bull bars, spare wheels (2) in place of one rear seat, steel hubs (all wheels), strengthened suspension, spare fuel tank, emergency tools and first aid kit, GPS sensor, 3mm aluminium sumpguard and under-body protection plate, extra front spotlights, extra tow loops (front and rear), supplementary engine starter switch, 'Thule' storage box attached to roof, extra cigar socket for powering equipment and an anti-theft 'tracker' device.

Which Way Next?

"Ah yes, " said Hanspeter, when I raised the subject, "I'm sure we can do something with SOS Children's Villages."

"What's SOS Children's Villages?" I asked politely.

"It's a charity which builds 'family-based' environments for children all over the world," explained Hanspeter, already tapping on his computer to search for their website.

"It was started by an Austrian humanitarian after World War II, and later expanded into Asia after the Korean War, with the idea of providing somewhere for orphaned and destitute children to be brought up with proper housing, schooling and direction."

Aha, I have noted another Korean connection.

The website reveals more. SOS Children's Villages is indeed a more-than-worthy charity with 'village' sites for orphaned children dotted across many countries of the world including, it turns out, not only South Korea, but also China and in some of the former Soviet Union countries like Azerbaijan and Uzbekistan – all of which are along the route we are now planning to take.

"Perfect," said Hanspeter, "you can leave that to me. I know the SOS Children's Villages' director over at Innsbruck and I will ask to see him, I'm sure he would want to bring their organisation in on this."

"But let's not forget GM Daewoo," chimed in Eric who has been following the conversation intently. "We have centres right across Europe which would want to see your car and hope to get some publicity out of this. That's the main thing we want from our deal remember!"

And so the pieces of our jigsaw continued to fall into place.

We consult the GM wall map to find the business centres where Daewoo, for its commercial reasons, would want us to call: Breda (Belgium/Holland), Paris (France), Milan (Italy), Munich (Germany), Vienna (Austria), Budapest (Hungary), Athens (Greece) and, of course, the starting off point at Luton (UK) and the finish at Seoul in South Korea.

"That's terrific!" I exclaimed. "If we add in the villages where SOS may want us to go, we'll have a dozen or more stopovers along our route. It will help us raise money for them, hopefully get some publicity for you, and give us a chance to stretch our legs!"

The hours spent in Zurich had been more than worthwhile. "Yes, a real breakthrough," Eric later agreed.

By the end of it, what had begun as a dream and a "crazy idea" had begun to look as if might actually happen. The Swiss, and soon my team back in the UK, now had a plan of when we would go, when we hoped to get there, how we would travel, and even where we would stop along the way. Oh, and how we could also raise money for some of the worst cases of children-in-need around the world.

It had been a remarkable day!

A few days later, back in the UK, I called a meeting for the "home" team at my house. It would probably be the one and only time for us all to get together before we left and I reckoned it was time for some personal bonding.

It's the Easter Bank Holiday weekend – a good time for a meeting if you have a full-time job in the week. Mediaman can't make it but the others, Tony the Snapper, from Brighton, Phil, who will be my co-driver, from Liverpool, and Angela, a friend from the publishing world who lives nearby, all arrive safely. Tony, all huff and puff, is an incredible one-and-a-half hours early, his arms full of papers and maps and a shoulder full of cameras. There's a bottle of wine in his bag, a box of chocolates and some bake-in-the-oven bread! It says a lot about him.

It's a good meeting, even if we are only four. More than anything, I just want us all to get to know each other because, like every team, in order to look out for one another we need to care for one another. It doesn't take long for the barriers of social shyness to come down. Phil is great. He's younger than the rest of us – at 25, a good deal younger in fact. ("Hey, I have a daughter your age", I am tempted to say – although I don't.) He's intelligent, has a witty style of understated conversation, and a streak of the rebel in him which all of us need for an adventure like this. Tony, very picky and seemingly weighed down with the detail and worry of it all, takes time to come out of his shell, while Angela (also known as Blue Carrot after her big blue chunky pen) is easy-going, open and friendly, and has soon made friends with everyone.

So this is the core of the team. And I feel like I have picked them well.

Which Way Next?

"At the end of all of this," I call them to order, " you Phil, Tony and me might all get to be celebrities! And you Blue Carrot will be the person who keeps us all together."

I can see my words sink in; the reality comes across their eyes. It's actually going to happen – the start of an adventure into the unknown. It's the kind of thing that changes lives forever and right now it's heading our way – not in a dream, but in a Daewoo.

We talk a lot. And laugh a lot too. But there is also some serious business to be attended to.

We list our responsibilities - including Geoff's as if he were here - so that everyone is clear on what they are expected to do: co-driver Phil will also be navigator and companion (how I shall come to rely upon him!); Tony, photographer and mechanic (a good guy to have in the back seat even if for only a limited time, with his chocolates and good humour); and Angela (the comfort of home, a friendly voice on the mobile phone and someone to keep us all motivated if spirits get low).

Our main business is to agree on the journey plan.

A start date, to suit everybody, has already been decided. And I have been able to bring them news from Switzerland about the GM Daewoo centres across Europe and about the children's Villages of our charity partners. OK, so that's where we'll have our checkpoints. But how long will it take to reach them? How many miles? What sort of problems?

Ah, where's that crystal ball?

By the end of the session we have done our best, drawn our line across a map on the table, checked with our books, pooled our knowledge, argued our opinions, unscrambled our thoughts.... and there it was: the provisional route of our adventure is laid before us for the very first time.

I email our plan to Hanspeter first thing next morning.

Chapter 6
THE KARAOKE KID

THINKING back to the team selection, my most crucial choice was always going to be Phil.

As co-driver he would take his turn at the wheel as we trundled off around the world. But there would be so much more to it than that. And I guessed we both knew it.

We talked about it after the team meeting. Being map-reader and navigator, it would be his responsibility to keep us on the right road ahead. And as the one and only on-board mechanic, he would need to make up for my pathetic lack of knowledge if the car developed problems.

Then he would have to help me record the stories of any adventures which came our way – taking the pictures after Tony, our Snapper, had left to return to his day job, answering questions along with me at the variety of press and publicity receptions which were to be arranged, and helping to send back our progress reports to base.

Those were the obvious things - and yes, he quickly agreed, he was happy to handle all of them.

But would we get on? That was the real question.

This Challenge was no leisurely weekend expedition off to the beach – this was being cooped up with another human being inside one little car through goodness-knows-what kind of dramas in all kinds of weird and not-so-wonderful places for 80 days – *á la* Jules Verne. There would be no-one else to make us laugh, nobody else's conversation to keep us entertained. Nowhere else to go and no-one else to turn to. Whatever happened, it would be just him and me, sharing the experience.

I knew the same questions were going through his mind.

"Well, what do you reckon?" I asked when the moment seemed right.

He looked at me for a while, slowly cocked his head, and then broke into a grin.

"I can't think of anyone else I'd rather do it with," he said.

So there it was, sink or swim. Another big decision made.

Which Way Next?

I had first met Phil at a Chinese New Year's Eve party at Sunderland University. Even now, it seems strange to think about the coincidence of it all. Never before had I been to something like that. In fact, I probably couldn't have said when the Chinese New Year was if you'd asked me – and I wasn't too sure where Sunderland was either.

But after all this is over I want to go to China to teach and write a book, remember? That's the connection. The university at Sunderland is taking me on as a kind of "honorary graduate", to go and teach in Nanjing at one of their partner colleges. So when the organisers in the Chinese Department asked me if I'd like to come to their party, I felt I should.

It turned out to be a wonderful night. More than 400 Chinese students arrive every year to study at Sunderland because they want to learn English and because the university has done a good job over in China establishing a reputation for its hospitality and good teaching. For Sunderland, the city, it's a cultural thing; while for Sunderland, the university, all the extra income from foreign students comes in very handy to keep the place going.

On party night all the right professors turned up with their lady wives trying impossibly hard not to look conspicuous in their Western party dresses. The sober-suited city Mayor and his entourage of officials turned up too.

It was all rather jolly. The students put on some genuine Chinese entertainment of song and dance, we all exchanged gifts in the Chinese custom, the Mayor got up to say: "Thank you, on behalf of all the people of Sunderland …" and then we all tucked into dishes of sweet and sour something from the local takeaway which had that night celebrated its biggest-ever order.

Later on, when the Mayor had gone and the music had been twisted up a notch, I found Phil at the bar supping beer and we fell into easy conversation.

He was a graduate of the university with a master's degree, he said, and he had just returned from China after teaching for a year on one of those arranged trips with a partner college like the one lined up for me.

"What did you think of it over there?" I asked as we struggled to call for another beer at the crowded bar.

"Oh, you'll love it," he said. "It won't be like anything you've ever known before – but you'll love it." And we chatted on.

His style was easy, open and friendly. I knew I liked him straight away. I remember we talked about China and the university, and his home town of Liverpool – and football. He also seemed interested in me and in what I was doing and why I was there, and although it must have been obvious to him that I was roughly twice his age, he didn't let that get in the way at all.

After a while one of the prettier Chinese girls approached and quietly asked him something.

At first he seemed to protest, waving his hands as if to shoo her away. But I could tell he was only being coy and sure enough, his face soon cracked into a grin and he walked with her towards the stage.

"Hey," he called over to me, " this will be embarrassing – they want me to sing!"

He was back five minutes later to rapturous applause.

"What on earth was that?" I asked, having not understood one single word of the song and with my mouth hanging open in stupefied wonderment.

"It's an old Chinese folk song, sung in my best Mandarin with a Liverpool accent," he said with a nonchalance like it was something you hear every day in the smoky students bars of downtown Sunderland.

To be honest, it had sounded to me more like the noise a hyena makes when it howls in the night. But that obviously wasn't the way it came over to the Chinese. They cheered Phil like he was a superstar.

"But where did you learn it?" I continued in awe.

"Karaoke," he said, "they're just mad for it over there. You'll see."

And I think I knew then that we could become the best of friends.

After the party we had kept in touch by email. He wanted to read my last book. I asked him for advice about where I should visit when I went to Nanjing for my teaching. He decided to pitch off to China himself again for a spell and sent me a postcard. "People are friendly. Food is great. Couldn't be happier," he wrote.

And now, when the Challenge trip came, it hadn't been hard to decide to ask him along as my co-driver. I called him on the phone one night. The conversation went something like this ...

Me: "Hey Phil, I've got an adventure coming up."
Phil: "Great. Count me in."
Me: "No, wait a minute Phil. I'm being serious here. It will take the best part of three months. Can you get the time off work?"
Phil: "What work? There's none around Liverpool you know."
Me: "Don't you want to know what the plan is?"
Phil: "Oh, all right then, tell me."

I outline the idea of driving a Daewoo car from the UK all the way to South Korea. There's a short pause at the other end.

Phil: "That will mean you going through China, right?"
Me: "Yes, all the way across it."
Phil: "Well, you'll want someone who can sing karaoke then."

And that was it; another decision made. Welcome to the team, you Karaoke Kid.

For my part, I was already calculating that Phil's knowledge of the Chinese and their traditionally slow and frustrating ways could be the key to whether or not this whole madcap idea might actually come off.

The research I had been doing didn't exactly fill me with confidence. Getting through China – and I had assumed that if we wanted to get to Korea by car there would be no other way – was clearly going to be one big hassle. The Chinese authorities may have decided that at long last it is time for a change. But after centuries of doing things their own way, and with the minds of more than a billion people to be, well, re-adjusted shall we say, nothing much is going to happen overnight.

Entry permits, for example, come in six different versions and all of them take an age to get approved by the serried ranks of civil servants. Then there's the little matter of wanting to drive a car through the place. The Chinese only like tour parties in coaches, I had found, and they usually only get their permits and visas issued after months of problems and delays. Me and the Karaoke Kid in a Daewoo? Forget it. Most people can't even read the road signs.

In David Brayshaw's book *The Road To Beijing* – in which he recounts his journey five or six years ago from London to the Chinese capital in an old Austin Healey (the closest account I have found to an adventure like ours) – I read how in total frustration, and after months of fruitless requests for an entry permit, he simply drove up to a Chinese border post and refused to move his car until someone gave permission to let him in.

Such was the conspicuousness of the Healey, the international importance of his sponsors, and the considerable political fallout in prospect, that the authorities eventually relented. Nevertheless, David Brayshaw and his co-driver were forced to carry a government official, jammed in behind the front seats of the already-cramped cockpit, for the rest of the way.

Would we too have to play this same game of border brinkmanship? I wondered. It was surely only as a last resort.

I had consulted my inscrutable contacts at the Tourist Office in London. "If only you had someone who could speak Chinese," they said.

Ah, but now we do have someone. Now we have Phil, the one who can do Mandarin with a Liverpool accent. Get us a permit at once or he'll sing you into submission!

And yet. And yet. With just six weeks to go it wasn't the paperwork for China that came to worry us most. Like I've said, it was the epidemic, the plague called SARS.

Well that, a set of newly tested nuclear bombs, and an earthquake in Turkey, to be absolutely exact.

The outbreak of SARS – so-called because it's so much easier to say and probably a lot less alarming than Severe Acute Respiratory Syndrome - is now looking like a potentially severe threat to our driving ambitions.

I get the Sunday papers to check the latest. The epidemic of this pneumonia-like virus, which began in southern China, has now apparently killed more than 300 people and hospitalised over 4,000 around the world.

According to one heavy business paper I read, the effects on manufacturing and consumer demand could have an even greater impact than the terrorist outrage at the World Trade Centre in New York on 9/11 in 2001. It's that big.

Which Way Next?

Schools are being closed, holidays cancelled, hospitals overwhelmed, and, more to the point for us, the World Health Organisation is advising visitors to stay away from China for the next three weeks. Then, they say, they will review the situation in three-weekly cycles.

The consequences for our plans are obvious – and we don't have much time left.

Then there's the threat of nuclear bombs.

Just last week, the papers tell me, North Korea – yes, that same North Korea we shall want to drive through on the way to Seoul in the South – has admitted to the world, for the very first time, that it has an arsenal of nuclear warheads in full working order and it won't be afraid to use them (maybe even, oh my goodness, on their Americanised former countrymen next-door) unless George W. Bush takes their name off the "Axis of Evil" list of countries he doesn't like the look of.

"Oh dear," I'm thinking, "our triumphant welcome at the GM Daewoo factory in South Korea might be a little warmer than we're expecting."

Whatever next? Well, here's another story guaranteed to put the wind up any would-be traveller wanting to plot a peaceful course along the country lanes from Luton to South Korea: there's been an earthquake.

It's happened in Turkey, plumb on our route. It's brought havoc and destruction and killed more than 100 people, many of them schoolchildren. And as if that isn't bad enough, we learn from the news that another could strike at any moment.

I ring the Karaoke Kid. "Hey Phil, have you heard the latest?"

"No, what's that?"

I tell him about the earthquake.

"Wow," he says. "Earthquakes, a plague, nuclear bombs ... You wait 'til they hear me sing."

Que sera sera, I whistle, folding the papers away. Whatever will be, will be...

Chapter 7
SMALL IN THE EXTREME

AND NOW – oh this is going to be painful – I need to talk about cars again.

A summons has come from the boss of PR at GM Daewoo UK. Mediaman had been doing his stuff. Editors on the motoring magazines – those glossy collections of manly escapism which I normally notice (although never look into) parked in a neat row for eye-level reading at my local newsagents – have been ringing up to ask for a picture of me and the Kalos in time for their next editions.

To hacks more usually switched on by the big torque of a Lamborghini Gallardo and the cornering prowess of a Porsche Carrera, our story had evidently sparked an interest. Mediaman put it like this: "It's something different for them. Let's just say they are more than a little surprised at your choice of transport and they think you are certifiably insane."

There are five weeks left. We had already received a message from GM Daewoo to say that the actual Kalos to be used on our trip had been sent for "prepping" to their engineers in Belgium.

It was a Kalos Sports model we were told, turned out in a nice blue finish with safety air bags (oh, that's good) and with only 7,700 km on the clock (ah, that's good too – how nice to know someone else has made sure it actually works). The experts in Antwerp were busy putting bars on the front in case we run into a bull (oh, really?), installing an extra fuel tank and spare tyres (that's comforting) and reinforcing the underneath bits.

But the car is in Belgium and that's no use for the British motoring press, said Mediaman. They want a picture of me and the car, and they want it now.

So off I go to Luton in Bedfordshire, which happens to be the centre of the universe for GM Daewoo UK, for an appointment with a photographer and my first real date with a stand-in Kalos, my beautiful Greek lady with a nice blue finish, which looks like the one in Belgium only without the new bits yet, if you see what I mean.

Which Way Next?

The weather is pure Bedfordshire in spring: all grey skies, pattering rain and a blustering wind. The photographer is hardly in the league of celebrity paparazzi and the venue is not exactly a film lot from a Hollywood blockbuster. But more of that soon.

For the uninitiated, and without putting too fine a point on it, Luton, the town, has seen better days. Once, for a century and more, it was a thriving place based on its famous reputation as a centre of hat-making. And even when the fashion for men in straw boaters had floated away, they still had Vauxhall, one of Britain's oldest car-makers, spread all over town.

But just as hat-making had come and gone, so also, much more recently, has Vauxhall, victim of a decision by General Motors (yes, they own that too) to close their manufacturing plant there after a long and ultimately losing battle against the cheaper labour costs of production at many of its competitors. The economic consequences have gone through the place like a cleaver.

Today, the town's last remaining claim to fame is through its airport – the base for one of the UK's better-known discount airlines which every year ferries millions of tourists to some of the hotter spots of Europe.

It isn't the kind of place many people would describe as the most romantic scene to come home to.

The airport sits high on a hill hardly more than a runway's length or two from the centre of town, and my brother, the pilot, who occasionally flies in here with a competitor airline, says it is known in the business rather disparagingly as "a lump on the bump."

Lorraine Chase summed up its disenchantment perfectly. The cockney television actress helped make the place famous in the 1970s with this memorable two-liner in a long-running ad for Campari:

"Were you wafted here from Paradise?" she is asked.

"Naaah, Luton airport," comes the unforgettable reply.

On my photo-shoot opportunity day, the town seemed more like the "sad and boggy place" described by Eeyore in A.A.Milne's *Winnie the Pooh*.

GM Daewoo's headquarters, which is just down from the airport, has brought life again to what was once a part of the old Vauxhall collection of buildings. But too many of the rest of them – office blocks, huge manufacturing sites, service centres and warehouses units – stand empty and forlorn in this grey and overcast weather.

Ironically, I discover that I am almost in the same place where just a year ago I came to give a talk about my last book to an assortment of local business folk in Vauxhall's old sports and social club. We had huddled there for lunch in a screened-off corner of an enormous meeting hall where I imagined many of the staff get-togethers had been held in those increasingly fraught and gloomy days as the company's closure plans were announced.

Afterwards, I had stopped for a chat with some of the ladies who prepared the lunch.

"It's so sad," said one, "after today's function we have some bookings for a few wedding receptions and then this place will shut. After all these years I don't know what I'm going to do."

I wished I could find her again today. Today I will tell her I am here again at the invitation of General Motors – albeit on behalf of GM Daewoo, their latest acquisition. The new regime is already doing well, I've been told. Production over in South Korea has been doubled and the cars are selling well. In the UK plans are under way to build a network of 150 franchise dealerships. Who knows, if everyone goes out and buys a Daewoo after hearing about our trip, the dinner ladies at the Luton sports and social club will get their old jobs back and maybe all these empty buildings will be full once more with rows of gleaming new Kalos cars with a nice blue finish.

Anyway, here at last was the moment. We came round the corner and there she was, my stand-in Greek Goddess waiting patiently for me in the centre of a vast and abandoned car park. And she looked … well … rather wet, and rather small.

It was a Friday, by all accounts a busy day down in the camera shop in Brighton, so Tony, our very own Snapper and soon-to-be back seat passenger, was sorry but he couldn't get away. He should have been happy. Instead we had Pete on one of his less glamorous assignments, with a large and impressive camera strung round his neck, a set of mobile steps for climbing up and down "to get the best angle, dear boy", and a disconcerting facial twitch which was undoubtedly not something he wanted.

"Ah, there you are," said Pete, ushering me over to where he planned his first shot.

He obviously wanted to get on with it.

In no time he was already halfway up his ladder, twitching furiously, and struggling under a large umbrella, which gave me the distinct impression that at any minute he might take to the air, like a latter-day Mary Poppins.

But first I needed to meet my date.

"Can you hold on a minute?" I asked walking over to the car, "I'd like to take a closer look at her before we start."

In all honesty, I think the first thing that struck me about my new Greek Goddess was that she looked rather like a wedge of blue cheese, chopped off at the back and chiselled down to a slice at the front.

And she did seem rather small.

I could imagine going down to the shops in south Luton in her ... but not so obviously to the shops in South Korea.

I walked all round her. Mentally I kicked her tyres. I opened the door, sat in the driver's seat, caressed her wheel. Looking down, I surveyed the dashboard. Yes, she certainly seemed to have gadgets and dials in all the right places. I glanced around. Yes, the seats looked nice and comfortable too.

But she did seem rather small.

Pete was waving at me with his free hand from the top of his ladder, holding the umbrella in the other like a parachute. Oh God, any minute now and I had visions of him jumping.

Inside the car I peered through the windscreen into the gathering gloom - thinking ahead, visualising what it would be like to spend three months of my life inside this machine, relying on it each and every day, listening to it purr, mile after mile, with no word of complaint.

"Maybe, just maybe, I am completely mad," I found myself thinking.

Pete came over to the driver's window and broke my concentration.

"Better get started," he said, twitching. "Looks like more rain on the way."

"What do you think of her?" I asked as he pointed his fishbowl camera lens at me and said 'smile'.

"Er…," he cleared his throat nervously, "well she does seem rather small."

Later, in the comfort of GM Daewoo's offices and with a cup of coffee in my hand, I am trying to make some sense of it all. Well no, let's be real, above everything else I am trying not to be worried.

This the 21st century, I am telling myself. This is men-on-the-moon time, and petrol stations, and credit cards and breakdown trucks, cellular phones and websites and sponsorship by the world's biggest car-maker who will surely make it their business to rescue us if we happen to arrive unexpectedly in a ditch somewhere on the way to the shops in South Korea.

And then I am thinking about what has happened before.

What about Prince Scipione Borghese and his journey from Peking to Paris in 1907? Of the five cars that started roughly 100 years ago, four of them made it. So what am I worried about?

And then there's that more modern account: In 1997, in the anniversary re-run of that original rally, nearly 100 cars set out on the Peking-Paris journey. Eighty-two of them made it – including a 30-year-old Volvo Amazon with the novelist Rosie Thomas on board. I calculate the odds to be better than eight out of 10 – so who dares to say I can't do it in a Daewoo?

But my beautiful blue Greek Goddess does seem rather small.

"Isn't there anything a little larger in your range?" I asked Sarah, the PR girl, as she passed by.

"Well, we have a 4 x 4 off-road vehicle called Scope," she said. My eyebrows shot up. "But there's only one of them so far. It's a prototype and not in production." My eyebrows shot down.

"But look, don't worry, the Kalos is a great little car and it's as good as anything we've got to get you there."

She presses a nice glossy brochure into my hand with a nice glossy picture of my latest date on the front. Inside, there is a piece headed up: "The Daewoo Kalos – a new drive."

It reads: "Our designers have been working around the clock to create their vision for the next generation small car. Bold and attractive, the Kalos strikes a balance between elegance and functionality. Greek for "beautiful", Kalos represents a fusion between small car practicality and multi-purpose vehicle (MPV) styling."

Oh, well, that's all right then, I'm thinking. We can certainly do with the practicality - although I'm not so sure about the fusion.

I flipped over some more pages and find lots of other glossy photos – nice pictures of ladies inside the car wearing fashionable sun glasses with wind in their hair, and space on the seats for handbags and shopping in the back.

It wasn't quite the image I had in mind for the journey ahead.

Further on I read some more: "Whether you are battling the daily chaos of urban life or taking a well-deserved break, driving a Kalos brings you complete peace of mind. Our Daewoo engineers worked overtime to deliver a car that would perform and protect in all types of weather … you'll feel safe and secure whatever the conditions."

Ah, that's reassuring – and I think of our own Kalos car, now being worked on in overtime by those nice Daewoo engineers over in Belgium. "Let's go big on the 'peace of mind' guys," I find myself muttering.

The section is headed up: "Testing cars to the extreme". And suddenly the penny drops –

Of course! So that's why Daewoo are kindly letting Snapper, the Karaoke Kid and me have their car for this journey of ours. We are merely guinea pigs – laboratory rodents in a social experiment of global transportation.

I can see it all. This whole thing is a put-up job – the truth is that they want to see how the car will perform on an extreme shopping expedition to the other side of the world!

Chapter 8
A GODDESS AMONG WOMEN

AND talking of the other side of the world.... the master route map on the wall of my spare bedroom had by now taken on the look of a plate of spaghetti. A plate of spaghetti that had had a drink or two more than it should have. With barely two weeks to lift-off for our 16,000-kilometre jaunt, I had evidence enough of the human and political complications of this extraordinary world of ours right there on my wall.

Strange to think that in this tiny, three square metre cubby-hole at my end-of-terrace in the ancient coaching town of Newport Pagnell – which I had now called, in all modesty, our World Headquarters – we should be master-minding a global campaign. But that's the way it was.

For those not in the know (and hardly anyone was) I can now happily reveal that the intelligence centre at World HQ was in reality an ancient personal computer with Samsung SyncMaster 3 printed on the front. I know that without consulting my notes because I had been seeing rather a lot of it in recent weeks.

It has no hard disk capacity and a memory almost constantly bordering on overload. There was also another little sign on the frame I noticed which said "low radiation" and which I had been thinking lately was probably a very good thing.

It had certainly never seen anything like what was now going on. And neither had I. Up to 50 emails a day were flashing before my eyes as the PR offices and agents and representatives of the global giants we had tumbled into bed with, roused themselves from their slumbers in the rush to gain themselves maximum publicity and maximum windfall revenue out of our adventure.

But where exactly were we going? On the wall, my spaghetti-like route plan bore the look of one of those "message trees" with all its branches hung about with sticker-notes detailing the latest news of where we were meant to go, when and why.

The itinerary was becoming exciting, if somewhat overwhelming.

Our stopovers, it seemed, were already being turned into jamborees with press conferences, official welcomes and civic receptions being arranged. At one place, in Budapest, I think, I had been invited to make a speech in the presence of the Hungarian Ambassador, no less.

Another sticky note told me that somewhere in Central Asia we could expect to receive an agency man who wants to make a documentary film of the trip and plans to hitch a ride with us through some of the more scenic parts of our route. We have visions of a man parachuting down in secret agent-fashion with a natty line in video kits strapped around his waist.

At many of the stopovers there are to be cheque presentations of money raised for SOS Children's Villages. Holland has sent one of the more memorable messages saying they will be launching a spot-the-Kalos competition inviting keen-eyed supporters across the nation to nip out and photograph our Greek goddess as we drive past – and win themselves a prize.

Our team is getting into the swing of things.

Over at Geoff's office - now known as the World Media Centre, but in truth a dusty one-room empire above a parade of shops in sleepy Stony Stratford High Street – press calls have been coming in from all over the place.

Mediaman, in our new and unassuming way, has decided he should be called "base commander" when the trip gets under way. Like the rest of us, he is finding this fame business a lot of fun to handle.

Peter, our official, twitching photographer, has lately been up and down his ladders more times than is good for him. I have been busy writing copy, giving radio interviews and dragging old journalist friends down to the pub (without much resistance) to, er, fill them in with the background story of our adventure. And Phil, innocently shy of all these things, has forced himself onto Page Three of his local paper up in Liverpool.

And we haven't even gone yet!

Meanwhile, back at the route map, those human and political dimensions, otherwise known as world events, have been taking root.

Be warned! No-one, but no-one, who might ever be thinking of planning an epic journey in the company of a Greek Goddess should ever under-estimate what problems our wondrous community of nations will set before them.

Phil, whose tasks include organising visas and entry permits, has spent two full weeks in London trying to cut through more red tape than you'll find in Santa Claus's packaging department at Christmas. "This is driving me nuts," he exasperated one day after an especially frustrating time at the embassy of somewhere or other from eastern Europe. And it got worse.

At the North Korean embassy, representing the world's last remaining Stalinist regime and opened only very recently in a neat semi-detached house in Ealing Common to a fanfare of car-horns from outraged neighbours, the gaggle of officials were surprised to see him. In fact, they were surprised to see anyone at all.

According to our over-burdened route plan we will be driving through North Korea on our way to Seoul in the South on the very last leg of our triumphant journey. But this didn't cut any ice with the baggy-suited servants of Pyongyang.

"We've no chance there," said Phil, reporting back to World HQ on his mobile phone.

"The embassy is not in the habit of issuing many tourist visas," he was told. Perhaps not surprisingly for a country which has recently been testing nuclear warheads, threatening the West with Armageddon if it doesn't keep its distance, and generally telling the world to mind its own business, they are rather suspicious about why anyone should actually want to go there voluntarily.

So that's the first certain deviation to Route 1 then. We'll have to put the car on a ferry and avoid North Korea by sailing right past it. I draw another line on the spaghetti tree.

Then there's China.

Now China is not the easiest place to get permission to drive through, even on ordinary days. For a start, they want to put an official guide in the car to help with signpost reading. Then there's some business about them being afraid visitors might see something they don't want, or listening to conversations they can't understand, or wearing sunglasses when the sun isn't out.

All in all, it's a bit of a hassle.

And that's at the best of times. But now is not the best; SARS is currently killing Chinese citizens in alarming numbers (the toll has risen to 700 deaths and 7,000 hospitalised cases at the most recent count) and China is being blamed for the spread of SARS to the rest of the world.

Which Way Next?

Most people, it seems, want to keep out of China. But not us. "We have an urgent date with the shopkeepers in Seoul and we would like to come through your country to reach them now please," Phil told them as forcibly as he could.

The story is a long one, but the outcome after much wrangling, and despite a rendition of his best Mandarin folk songs with a Liverpool accent, the imperturbable officials at London's Chinese embassy failed to be swayed by the antics of the Karaoke Kid.

"You must wait for sickness stop," was their velly, velly final answer.

Ah, but here comes a message from Daphne, otherwise known as General Motors' queen of administration at the Shanghai office (and yes, you don't find anyone much better placed to unstick the red tape in China than Daphne):

"We can get you a driving pass and a guide, but I'm afraid the price is rather high," she said.

"Oh? What's high," I asked nervously.

"25,000 dollars US," she said, even more nervously.

"Twenty-five thousand dollars!" I spelled it out slowly and with an incredulous alarm in my voice.

"Daphne, do you realise, that's about three times what the car is worth and more than half the total money we hope to raise in sponsorship! Are they thinking of blocking off the side roads and giving us a police escort all the way through?"

"It certainly seems like that," she said. "It's probably best that you just set off and we try to sort this out for you on the way. There are provisionally six or seven weeks until you reach China so maybe the SARS thing will have died down by then."

Ah, so that's another likely diversion to Route 1 on the spaghetti map: avoid China, turn left at Kyrgyzstan, and go over the top of it through Kazakhstan, Mongolia and Russia. We could have just added another 2,000 miles and another week to our journey, I reckoned.

Mind you, would we even get to Kyrgyzstan?

News filtering back to World HQ from Phil, as he does his marathon trek around the London embassies, is not so good.

Turkmenistan, the country east of the Caspian that we would most likely go through to reach Kyrgyzstan, is not letting anyone in just now, he reports. The place is run by President Turkmenbashi (full name Sapamurad Niyazoz Turkmenbashi the Great, Father of all Turkmen) and he is going through a rather unhelpful patch apparently. After taking it upon himself to re-name the days of the week and the months of the year, and to declare some astounding growth figures for his country's economy, he has now decided that no foreigners should be able to see for themselves the benefits of his fine country.

I looked at the spaghetti map. So which other way then? Turn to the south?

Iraq, devastated by the effects of the recent war, and Iran, thought to be next on America's "Axis of Evil" list, look like the best ways round to the south of the Caspian.

Ugh! I draw another line on my message tree and put details of the diversions into a file marked "Contingency planning for world events."

Already there are reports in there about earthquakes in Turkey, a collection of travel warnings from the British Foreign Office, and an assortment of discussion papers on the danger to foreigners from terrorism in post-Soviet Russia.

I stick another note on the spaghetti tree. "Which way next?" it simply said.

Finally, just a week before leaving, we meet another hero in this madcap adventure.

Let me tell you more.

Yves Fourdin is waiting for us at the GM Daewoo HQ in Luton. He is a slight figure, just turned 40; a lean whippet of a man with close-shorn hair and a slash of dark moustache across his upper lip in the Poirot style, and he is standing, just like a detective on guard duty, beside our little Greek Goddess – the real one this time.

The Karaoke Kid had been twittering all the way here about what she would look like.

I did my best to describe her. "She will be rather small," I warned.

"But beautifully formed I hope," he countered, "and not too small either. I sneaked a look at one in my local garage the other day. She'll be just fine. No problem."

Anyway, here she is – no stand-in starlet this time, but the real Miss McCoy. She has been in Yves' hands for the last month at his workshop in Belgium. He is, I now know, what is described in this business as a "prepper" – an engineer charged with the responsibility of preparing a car to survive an exceptional amount of wear and tear, and which, in our case, means using every bit of his knowledge to guarantee our safe motoring.

He is also, we quickly learn, a former national rally champion of Belgium, who now runs a famous repair and engine-tuning shop near Antwerp and who has been hired at the expense of GM Daewoo to spend 300 hours of prepping time on our goddess.

The transformation is remarkable. She is still small, it is true, but now her sleek blue flanks have been etched with stick-on slogans and there's a line down each side that starts with London and ends with Seoul. It goes up and down in irregular fashion and reminds me of those blood pressure charts that doctors put at the foot of hospital beds.

On top she has a luggage container bolted to the roof which, in an imaginary moment, I can conceive as a lady's hat perched on her head like a bonnet (if you'll pardon the pun) at Easter, and a concoction of metal bars at the front, apparently for the purpose of fending off any marauding bulls which happen to get in our way, but which look to me for all the world like a seductive mouth of smiling lips.

The little girl has been turned into a robust and sophisticated woman by this prince of mechanics.

We take a tour with our new-found hero.

Beefed-up suspension, strengthened shock absorbers, extra lights which poke out like frog's eyes on sticks and peer into the distance behind protective grilles, a 3mm sheet of reinforced aluminium welded onto her body underneath, chunky tyres with "steel-belted" stamped across them … here is a woman who can surely take care of herself.

"Hey, you like my baby?" queries Yves, as though he is demonstrating something from the smaller range of Chieftain tanks.

And now we look inside.

"I have made her strong, like a good woman!" he laughs, "but I make her still feminine and still a car. No?"

He lifts up the rear door of the hatchback. "Now you see this."

Inside the area where the boot space should have been, Yves now uncovers what Aladdin would have called his treasure cave.

"Inside this one," says Yves, lifting up a kind of metal-plated trapdoor, "I have put the spare fuel tank."

We look at, well, an extra fuel tank, installed with a pump on top and lots of pipes and tubes attached.

"You will be glad of this when the next fuel station is 500 km away," he says with a laugh that made me a little more nervous than perhaps I should have been.

And now he lifts out a big metal box, which had been held to the floor at the back with thick straps of webbing. "These are my jewels," he says.

He opens it up as if he were a conjurer about to perform on stage and he brings out every item one by one with a magician's flourish. A pack of spanners, screwdrivers, pliers, gauges, bulbs, fuses, a wheel jack and handle ... a packet of clips, some tubes and hoses, extra wires, a spare pump, bottles of fluid for this and that, tie wraps, stretchy straps, plugs and filters ...

Soon the ground around us is festooned with enough motoring equipment to hold a car boot sale. He has followed the Noah's Ark principle – two of everything.

Each item is examined and everything explained. The Karaoke Kid and I are mightily impressed. Or, at least, we would have been until I spotted something in a plastic bag, which our prince of mechanics seemed to have missed.

"What's this?" I asked, holding it up to him in all innocence.

"Ah," (was that a small kink in the Belgian's moustache I noticed?) "that's a tow rope."

There was a rather prolonged silence after that.

We say our goodbyes in the office. Yves will be driving back to Antwerp in the empty transporter van in which he brought our goddess over. After a month of living with her day and night I imagine he will feel rather lonely.

We have spent more than two hours with him poking and prodding our new partner, twisting her knobs and flicking her switches. To be honest, for a motoring agnostic like me, the whole experience has been located somewhere on the high side of overwhelming. But I still venture the question: "Is there anything else you need to tell us, Yves?"

He takes out a small visiting card and writes on the back:

Which Way Next?

"Here," he says, "this is my mobile phone number. You can call me anytime from anywhere..."

I think he thought this final gesture would be rather comforting. But, to tell the truth, it wasn't. Like the tow rope he had forgotten to mention, it only served to concentrate my mind on what could go wrong.

With less than a week to go before the Great Departure, the atmosphere is now a heady mixture of expectation, unavoidable decision-making brought on by the imminent deadline, and a severe dose of blind panic.

There are several last-minute hiccups. Gallingly, since we are being funded by one of the world's largest companies, a delay over the sponsorship contract leaves me holding a sizeable personal bank overdraft. The money is a best-guesstimate to cover all our costs, and over at the World Media centre Mediaman is muttering darkly that the 'value' of publicity already achieved has exceeded their sponsorship budget by a wide margin.

There is late drama too on the political front when Kazakhstan – a key country if China stays closed – finally initiates our visa approval process. Just one working day remains when a fax arrives telling us to get the application into their London embassy and the Kid finds himself under suspicion from a startled station-master when papers and a packet of money are handed to him through the window of a London-bound train.

But he makes it there with all of an hour or two to spare.

Back at my house, now being readied for renting out, the office of our World headquarters is being wound down. Or, to be more precise, the spaghetti map on which we have stuck our plans for this adventure has been put in one cardboard box, and our low-radiation communications centre has been put in another, and both have been dispatched to the loft.

So this is it then. It's time to go.

Chapter 9
CLEARED FOR LAUNCH!

WEEK ONE: If I'm honest, the big blast-off, when it came, was more low-key than high octane.

Maybe there had been too much hype. Or maybe too much hope. Or maybe it was just that Luton isn't quite familiar with this kind of thing.

Geoff's efforts at the media centre had already scored major publicity hits about our impending adventure in everything from the posh motoring magazines to the mass circulation *News of the World* with its topless starlets and naughty vicars – and quite often a combination of both – and clippings from papers have been coming in from Spain to South Korea and from Chingford to China.

"Even if some of the headlines poke fun at the unlikelihood of anyone in their right mind attempting such a journey in a Daewoo – and a tiny one at that – well then who's to care?" he said. And no-one seemed to disagree.

But if our crazy expedition had suddenly become publicity flavour of the month, Luton, unfortunately, had not.

To be fair, the newly resurgent headquarters of GM Daewoo UK is only in its infancy, with offices tucked up a service road behind a couple of dusty factory sites. And the hastily-erected banner hanging from the entrance gate isn't exactly what we had in mind for the launch of our "world first" event.

But never mind.

Inside, an odd assortment of local journalists, PR people, representatives of GM management, a well-meaning lady from SOS Children's Villages, and the crew from an Asian TV station, are ushered into a small conference room for orange juice and biscuits, to hear a brief outline of our plans, to ask a series of, well, not such serious questions, and to witness the handing over of one of those giant polystyrene cheques which look rather better in publicity pictures than the real ones where the figures are too small to read.

Things perked up a bit outside.

Thankfully, I find I have remembered to pack my Elton John outfit from a recent fancy dress party. It may not be the usual get-up for adventurers about to risk life and limb on a car journey of marathon proportions, but for occasions when, shall we say, spirits need a bit of lifting, it can do the trick. So on goes the wig, the star-burst dark glasses and giant $ medallion, and the surprise appearance of our secret celebrity guest goes down a treat.

Mediaman, Blue Carrot and twitching Pete are there in the crowd and the sun comes out from behind a cloud right on cue to wish us well. The entire Daewoo workforce abandon their desks and form a guard of honour in the forecourt as managing director Andy Carroll waves a Union Jack in grand prix style to send us off.

Snapper Tony, committed to us for the first two weeks, climbs into the back, and the Kid, his arms stacked with maps and charts and his head full of the techno-jargon of mobile phones and laptops, sits beside me at the wheel. A twist of the key and the Greek Goddess, GG for short, sparks into life.

Hey, it's really going to happen – our great journey on this bright and breezy Monday morning in the ninth day of June has begun.

I think we were somewhere around Colchester when we first noticed it. The smell of petrol that is. It was only the middle of the day but I was already getting that kind of woozy feeling more normally reserved for chucking-out time at the pub on Friday nights.

"Can anyone smell petrol?" I yelled above the din as our gang waved and hollered at a car-full of gawpers moving slowly past, while those inside it wondered what this strangely-decorated family hatchback was doing meandering along the country roads of Hertfordshire and Essex in the general direction of the port at Harwich.

"Aw, don't be daft, it's only because we've got so much of it on board," said the Kid.

But I wasn't so sure.

"Not even 100 miles gone and I reckon we've got a problem already," I said. And, oh heck, I was right.

The smell was still there when we collected the Goddess after our overnight trip on the ferry to Holland. In fact it was worse.

We drove on to Breda, where GM Daewoo's cavernous parts centre for the whole of Europe straddles the borders of Holland and Belgium,

Daewoo Challenge Photo Album

Part 1

Start: GM Daewoo UK Managing Director, Andy Carrol, sets the wheels in motion at Luton.

Finish: GM Daewoo Chief Executive Nick Reilly congratulates Richard and Phil at the official finish in South Korea. © pic: GM Daewoo

ORIGINAL THOUGHT: Only 15986km to go: Chief 'prepper' Yves Fourdin with Richard in Breda.

The Kalos celebrated its first birthday in Bangladesh, so the Challengers arranged a party for the youngsters at the SOS Children's Village, Dhaka.

Rome: Outside the Coliseum.

Bavaria: On the way to Imst in Austria.

Paris: Phil prepares for a photo-shoot beside the majestic River Seine.

Laos: Driving through the gloom.

Dhaka: Inside the ambulance.

Vietnam: New registration of 0001 as the Kalos makes history.

GG sets sail from Hios to Turkey.

Safety inside the plane at Dhaka.

Bangladesh: A Russian-made plane called Cinderella flew the Kalos to Thailand.

The Challengers had to call on other forms of transport along the way. There was a train (opposite) in Uzbekistan, a plane (below) in Afghanistan, another (overleaf) in Bangladesh, and a ferry from the Greek islands to Turkey.

Kabul: A wartime reminder.

Afghanistan: A 'mercy flight' by this Dutch crew saved the day.

Border Guards: in the sun in Pakistan and in the rain in Kazakhstan.

Where's that train? GG waits on the ramp to enter Uzbekistan.

Turkey: Among the minarets.

Uzbekistan: Visiting Samarkand.

Azerbaijan: Ancient and modern on the outskirts of Baku.

to fulfil our first publicity date and to receive another three polystyrene cheques for the children in need.

And it was still there.

"See what you make of this," I said quietly to the boss as I led him to the car when all the fuss had died down.

"Ah," he took one whiff. "I think you need to go and see Yves the prepper. You're in luck – he's no more than two or three hundred kilometres up the road near Antwerp."

"Yes, I know," I said rather ruefully, "he gave me his phone number only the other day. It's just that I was rather hoping I wouldn't have to use it quite so soon."

The vapour trail – which, come to think of it, is about the right description for our problem – leads us to Yves Fourdin's garage in a place called Att (or Ath, according to another signpost) in an area of Belgium where the residents are known somewhat disconcertingly as Walloons.

It is, I think, one of the shortest place names I can ever recall, but then Att (or Ath) gives every appearance of being a one horsepower town where most people would not want to stop for long.

Our prince of mechanics is obviously the local star. He has his garage set out on a semi-rural spot with an inside showroom featuring his winning rally cars, more trophies on display than you can shake a gearstick at, and a workshop out the back where we find him busy under the bonnet of another conversion job.

"Ah Richard," he says with a note of surprise, "I didn't expect to see you so soon."

"And neither did I," I said, "neither did I."

Well, in the end, after about an hour's poking and pulling about, the cause of our early crisis is identified. It is indeed the result of so much petrol being carried on board - which is leaving fumes from the spare tank trapped beneath his magician's box of just-in-case spare parts.

"Oh dear," says our Poirot look-alike, "you often get these difficulties when a car is adapted away from its normal state – but I am sorry it has happened so soon."

And he quickly got to work to create more "breathing space" for the petrol in that part of the car.

We climb back into the Goddess.

"Now are you sure that's the last we will see of you?" I joke from the window as we make for the road.

"Oh yes, you can count on it," he says.

But a little further on, when I pull down the sun visor against the glare, I notice he has stuck another of his business cards in the lining with his mobile number scribbled on the back.

Another early problem is communications. With a website to feed daily with stories and pictures, columns to write for sundry newspapers and progress calls to our next destinations, we had thought that our combination of mobile phones and laptops would be able to cope with the demand.

But we were wrong.

Or maybe we just weren't clued up enough technically, despite the Kid's master's degree in electronics and his skills at the keyboard.

"Is there anyone out there mother? Talk to me please …" says a woeful message from Mediaman, now doubling up as our base commander, after three fruitless days of trying to make contact. We find his email but we can't get the computer to reply to it because we aren't in a spot where, by all accounts, our phone is free to roam.

By day four, with the Kid engulfed in wires and modems and other computer peripherals, he disappears to his room in the small hotel we have stumbled on somewhere in central France, and joins us a couple of hours later with a smile of satisfaction on his face. Apparently he has hacked into the hotel's phone system to get a line out for his server to send messages.

No problem in that, we surmise … until we realise why *le patron* is looking rather glum. He wouldn't have known it, but the reason he hasn't had a single customer's call all evening is because his line has been permanently engaged.

There is a day too – in lovely Strasbourg at the end of our first week – when I want to compose another chapter for this very book. Maybe it is due to some electronic cross-border vagaries as our roadshow has wandered across several countries already, maybe it is down to our own inadequacies, maybe it is because so much of the equipment is new and untried by us …

I really can't say. But everything is so very changed from the comfort of our low-radiation intelligence centre at the World HQ back home that we often find ourselves struggling for ways of getting our information across the airwaves.

So on this day, in downtown Strasbourg, the Kid has to escort me to a convenient park bench in the centre of town where I sit all afternoon in the sunshine, surrounded by my papers and working with my laptop wired up to a spare battery from the car (a potentially valuable item which we have therefore cunningly hidden inside a dustbin liner in case of attack from, well, battery muggers, I suppose).

It makes for an unusual sight – but thankfully my concentration is broken only by the occasional drunk looking for somewhere to sleep off the afternoon's intake, by some lively children from a set of swings and roundabouts nearby, and by the owners of several stray dogs.

And so to the next stop in this first week of our expedition – and where better than Paris to receive our sophisticated GG with the bonnet on top?

GM Daewoo's French office near Charles de Gaulle airport plays host to another publicity and cheque handover session, choosing as the venue a splendid floating restaurant moored on the River Seine in the shadow of the magnificent cathedral of Notre Dame. As we drink champagne and make our speeches it is easy to think the world is a far better place than when we started.

We learn that the city has been gridlocked by traffic for days in the confusion caused by state workers marching in protest at their falling pension values. But today there is only the traditional mayhem of Parisian drivers roaring round the roads like there is no tomorrow.

Snapper, who was once a prepper himself in his racing car phase, has taken GG's wheel with relish and now delights in the local game of wing-mirror lottery – a speciality in this city where the simple rule is: drive as fast as possible and see how close you can get to someone else's wing-mirrors without actually knocking them off.

"You can keep Brands Hatch and Silverstone. I haven't had this much fun in years!" yells Tony as he wins us a few more bonus points in the game.

We make time too to see the sights, but after the Eiffel Tower and the

Which Way Next?

Arc de Triomphe we need to visit the Place de la Concorde in homage to that day, nearly a century ago, when the Italian prince rumbled into this place after his triumphant journey from Peking.

Back then there were crowds of thousands to greet the heroes, but today there is only us, parked precariously for a rapid photo-session in a corner of the massive square while the modern traffic swarms all around like angry wasps.

Just as we are leaving I see the two drop-dead-gorgeous PR girls from GM Daewoo's Paris office rather sheepishly handing Snapper some flat little packages, which he quickly slips into his bulky camera bag.

"Hey Tony, what have you got there?" I ask when I remember a little later in the journey.

He fumbles in the bag with embarrassment and pulls out a couple of packets of designer stockings.

"Wow, now this you have to explain," I say to him with a grin.

"Well it was like this you see - I was telling them how you can sometimes use stockings if your fan belt breaks, or if you need to filter out the dirt from petrol and …"

"Yeah, yeah," I finished the sentence for him, "what some blokes will do just to sniff the knickers of two pretty girls!"

All told, Week One had been a great start to the journey. We had held three publicity sessions, already received donations worth several thousand euros for SOS Children's Villages, overcome some early difficulties with the car and our communications systems, and been hosted in some of the nicest cities in Europe.

"Not bad for a little idea that only came up four short months ago," I said to the gang as we briefed up on our journey plan for the week ahead.

"But let's not forget that this is the easy bit. Europe is home for us, and we'll be very unlucky if something major goes wrong."

"So let's enjoy it while we can – because the hard stuff is still to come."

Distance driven so far: 850km

Chapter 10
THE RULES OF THE ROAD

WEEK TWO: There are, at a rough count, 15,150 kilometres still to go; in truth, we have hardly got beyond our own front door. Yet already we have visited six countries in the first week – leaving the UK, and passing through, variously, parts of Belgium, Holland, France, Germany and Switzerland on our stopover assignments.

In the week ahead we will visit two more – Austria and Italy. Besides further promotional dates with GM Daewoo, we also have the first two important engagements with SOS Children's Villages, and we shall need to put GG through more of her paces with a longish run down from the Bavarian Alps to Rome and back.

The first of our visits to the children's villages is at Diessen, a tiny hamlet built in the style of a German Hans Christian Andersen beside the picture-book mountain scenery of Lake Ammersee. It is a small cluster of homes, set in a wonderful place, which was established initially nearly 50 years ago through the gift of a lady benefactor, has been added to by the generosity of local land-owners, and is financed by well-wishers from across the world.

Today, nearly 100 children in the village are being given a roof over their heads, friendship, schooling, "parental" guidance by SOS mothers, and a clearer direction towards a better and more worthwhile future. Many of them turn out, especially for us, to sing songs of welcome and to accompany us, happy and laughing, on a tour of the site.

It is an inspirational day. The children, who are sent here by the German courts and authorities as being in need of care – and often protection – mostly have behavioural difficulties caused by the violent, sexual or psychological abuse administered by one or other of their parents.

Elsewhere in the world, SOS Children's Villages often busy themselves caring for the orphans of wars and conflict, but in its way what has happened to these children in Ammersee seems far worse.

Christoph Rublack, who is in charge of the village and is the guide for our visit, puts it more directly: "The sad fact is that if they were the victims of war, everyone would understand the problem better.

"But they are not; they are the victims of our wealthy and sophisticated society in western Europe in the 21st century. It is a growing and worrying trend."

For the next leg of our journey – a "double-header" of visits to the GM Daewoo centre in Rome and then to another SOS Village nearby, we must travel nearly 1,000 km.

Snapper is up and about organising an early-morning inspection. He will be leaving us in Rome to fly back to the camera shop and his other world in Brighton. But for the moment he is anxious to make sure that we follow his rules of the road.

There are six of them – all designed to make sure that our sweet little Goddess isn't hiding some dark secret ready to bring us grief on the way to the shops. I get the feeling he has drawn up the list especially for me.

"See this," he says pulling the dipstick out of its sheath like it was the Sword of Excalibur, "if the oil doesn't come up to this line here, you MUST do something about it. No oil equals no engine, and no engine equals no going anywhere. Got it?"

I said I had. Got it, I mean.

He points out other things to check each day, mostly to ensure that we have enough of them. There is the brake fluid reservoir. "If the level inside doesn't come up to this line here (he has drawn a line with a pen on the outside of the container) you will soon have no brakes. No brakes equals no stopping, and no stopping equals …" and he draws a line with his finger across his throat in a demonstration which looks suspiciously like the way to peel an Adam's apple without a knife.

And yes, I get the idea on brake fluid too.

All Snapper's rules are very similar. They are simple, important, and explained in short words, which even I can understand. "Do these things before you set off every morning and you will stay alive," he says. Instructions don't come much clearer than that.

There is even an explanation of how to use the stockings from those PR girls in Paris. And this time I notice his description is a lot more colourful and could surely only be attempted after an evening's intake of alcohol and the use of several mirrors.

But what nobody knew was that just an hour or two later all of us in the little GG would be suffering from something which certainly hadn't made Snapper's Top Six rules of survival, with or without wearing stockings.

We first began to realise that something wasn't quite right soon after crossing the border into Italy (not, I must quickly add, and especially for Italians, that their fine country had anything to do with it). No, the fact is, central heating knows no boundaries.

I had better explain.

It was turning out to be a fine day. In fact, a very fine day. After the cool of the Alps in Bavaria, and as the morning moved towards lunchtime, the weather grew better – and the sun grew hotter.

Not unnaturally, the Karaoke Kid, who was doing the driving at the time, turned on the air-conditioning.

"Hey, can anyone smell burning?" It was me again, asking the pressing question from the back. I had just been hit by a blast of air so hot it left me gasping.

Snapper, in the passenger seat, conducted a swift investigation of the knobs and dials. "Hmmm, that's strange," I hear him say as he twists them one way and then the other. Now he is working on the air vents, shutting and opening them one by one, and meanwhile accidentally unleashing another great roar from the furnace just when I'm least expecting it.

"Can't understand it," he declares at length, "the air conditioning unit seems to have gone into reverse and has decided it should turn itself into a central heating plant."

"Now OK," I hear myself say, "but this is Italy (no offence) and not the Sahara – so what's the problem with just turning it off and opening the windows to keep the car cool?"

So, of course, we try that too.

Never mind that I have turned the back seat into a kind of mobile office with all my writing stuff and pieces of paper now flying about in the car like we have just encountered a hurricane. This is not the time to get het up about anything.

Which Way Next?

No, the real problem is that the day outside is hotter than ever – so hot, we later discover, that it is, in fact, becoming the hottest day at this time of year in these parts than it's been for longer than most people can care to remember.

So I file my papers carefully on the floor under the spare wheel and we keep the windows open for a bit, but believe it or not, it's so hot out there we soon decide it's cooler to keep the windows closed than open ... which is really saying something considering there are three adult males shoehorned into this sauna bath of a car, stowed to the gunwales with luggage, spare wheels, an extra fuel tank, and enough spare parts to build a full-scale replica GG.

It's now mid-afternoon, we all weigh a bit less (and smell a lot worse) than we did when we got up today, there are still 400 km to go to Rome and we have to arrive there on time or our schedule will fall apart.

I decide to ring the base commander to ask his best advice.

But there's no sympathy there.

"You shouldn't be surprised," he says. "I'm pretty sure that nothing will have actually gone wrong with the AC system. Running it takes a lot of power from the engine. The poor little car is at the very limit of its strength to carry all of you and your kit and this is just its way of telling you that it is bordering on overload. Your best bet will be to carry on down to Rome as best you can and then get Daewoo's engineers to have a look at it."

I call up Yves, the mechanical wizard Walloon, and various other GM Daewoo people. But they all say something similar.

So that's it then, Snapper does some calculations on the back of a rather soggy piece of paper: there will be another three hours before we get to Rome and all we can do is just sweat it out.

But now comes another twist in this never-to-be-forgotten, airless, wood-fired pizza oven of a journey.

It happens, rather appropriately, in a place on the Italian A1 autoroute called Firenza and I imagine that those who witnessed it will have already converted its memory straight into legend.

Inside GG the temperature has risen to a level where I am seriously contemplating growing tomatoes as an alternative occupation to back-seat travel writing, but lately, as we have peered out through the steamed-up windows, it has become more and more evident to our gang of hotheads that something very significant is happening to the weather outside.

Perhaps it was because of the rapidly rising humidity; I'd need to check with a meteorologist – but very suddenly, in the middle of a previously blazing hot afternoon, the sky over Firenza turned into night, clouds swirled in from nowhere, giant gashes of lightning tore through the air and the rain literally thundered down, flooding the road in a matter of seconds and forcing all traffic to stop, willingly, for probably the first time ever in Italy (sorry again).

And there was worse to come – within minutes the rain had turned to golf ball size hail stones which thumped onto little GG's bonnet of a luggage-box hat and threatened to flatten it.

I suppose those who know about these things would call what happened a flash flood, or perhaps an Italian monsoon.

Never having seen anything like it before, the only thing I know is that for the first time in several sweaty, fetid hours our gang was mighty glad we had our windows up.

In a land which has witnessed more than its fair share of heavenly events and strange apparitions down the years, we took it to be a sign from the ancient Gods of Rome warning its citizens that we were about to arrive.

Sadly, Snapper has to leave us in Rome and head back to his camera shop. Despite our best hopes there is apparently no engineer available to fix the car, so we decide to return north to Austria with all GG's windows open in the cool of the night.

Distance driven so far: 3,700 km

Chapter 11
A DREAM COME TRUE

WEEK THREE: Driving in unknown cities abroad was always going to be one of the more daunting experiences in store for us. It's a universal problem in the more highly developed countries; there are just too many cars. The trauma is bad enough in London, but at least it is possible to read the road signs there, and most people get to know enough names and places to point their cars in roughly the right direction.

We have already had great trouble in Paris, where the surging tide of traffic swept us helplessly along this way and that until Snapper had the brilliant idea of navigating us out of the maelstrom with the help of a boy scout compass which he had thought to pack for just such an emergency at the very last minute in a bag marked "Other Things".

Now it is the beginning of the third week and we have encountered the same problem in Innsbruck.

Well no, not the same problem exactly, but similar.

Innsbruck is an Austrian city, so that makes it abroad. Neither the Kid nor I have been here before, so that makes it unknown. And while it is true to say that this polite and well-ordered place doesn't have the same volume of traffic as many other foreign cities, it is still pretty difficult to find where you want to get to when the time is after midnight and the road signs don't mean too much.

We are here to find the world headquarters of SOS Children's Villages. We have a breakfast date with Richard Pichler, their inspirational secretary-general and official *grand fromage* who wants to thank us personally for what we are doing.

But now we can't find it.

Up and down we go, round and round we go.

"Hey," I said to Karaoke as we passed a dimly-lit McDonald's, "I'm sure we've been this way once or twice already."

And we had.

Strangely, for a place so straight-laced as Innsbruck, I knew we had been this way before because the same ladies of the night were standing in their not-so-dimly-lit doorways further down the same street.

66

Being the driver at this point, Karaoke's eyes were firmly on the road. But mine weren't – and I recognised the city's source of final nightime entertainment from our last lap around ten minutes before when they had given similar laughs of disbelief as our little GG, resplendent in her full signage as a supporter of children's charity work, had sauntered slowly by.

Innsbruck, thank goodness, when you are as lost as we were, is not the largest of cities. So it didn't take long before we found ourselves back in the self-same street for at least the third time.

"OK," I said to the Kid, noticing the big blonde with the skimpy pink number putting her hands on her hips like this was no joke anymore, and signalling that she, at least, meant business. "I think it's time we got some help on directions."

And so it was that a local taxi driver on Innsbruck's red light run got his strangest-ever fare.

The grizzled old boy looked at me like I was three toots short of a yodel. He was parked rather ostentatiously further down the street making, I had no doubt, a very tidy living from ferrying punters backwards and forwards to this place well into the early hours.

"You want to go where?" he asked me to repeat the name of the children's organisation again because, well let's face it, he wasn't asked that kind of question too often in this part of town at this time of night.

"And you just want to follow me there?" His question bordered on disbelief, just as much disbelief, I imagined, as if I had told the big blonde with the skimpy pink number putting her hands on her hips that I only wanted to ask directions.

"Well yes," I said rather sheepishly.

Twenty minutes later, way across town, our strange miniature convoy drove into the front entrance of the SOS Children's Villages world headquarters. I saw the old boy looking at the Kid and me, then he checked their organisation's name on the side of our car and handed me rather more change than I was expecting.

His German was thickly accented, but I swear I heard him say something about a discount...

Mind you, there were more surprises when we made it down to breakfast next morning with Herr Pichler.

Unknown to the Kid and me, his entire staff of more than 50 had been summonsed to gather in a courtyard area outside the head office. The idea, it transpired, was for him to take us out to GG at the chosen moment and ask us to drive her around the corner where his team was waiting in a "guard of honour".

Then there would be the usual shaking of hands, an exchange of hearty good wishes, a speech or two, and a battery of cameras ready to record the moment.

The honour fell to me. "Please start her up," said the *Numero Uno*, "I would like to go with you around the front."

But, oh dear, GG hadn't read the script.

We found out later it was something to do with the fuel supply. The starter motor turned the engine over but it didn't fire. I tried again. Nothing. And again. Still nothing.

Ugh! Suddenly I had that kind of sinking feeling they must have experienced on the Titanic.

"Oh, that's not so good," said the secretary-general, "but never mind." And with that he jumped out of the car in an instant and, calling to a nearby colleague to give him a hand, the pair of them then pushed the car, with me inside steering, across the courtyard and up to the lines of waiting staff.

There is some laughter and then loud applause as, with one big heave, our powerless Goddess with her embarrassed driver is pushed into the entourage with a final flourish. The *grand fromage* has saved the day.

It was on the way up to Innsbruck when I learned the full history of how SOS Children's Villages began.

We had stopped at Imst, a tiny community in the Austrian Alps where soon after World War II Hermann Gmeiner, a farmer's son, had established the first of his villages as a refuge for orphans.

He had had the idea after witnessing the poverty and degradation suffered by countless thousands of children left without parents, and although he didn't have enough money to start the work himself he hit on the idea of sending a Christmas card appeal to everyone in the local phone book.

The land at Imst was donated by a well-wisher and enough money came in from the appeal to build the first house, ready for an SOS mother to bring up a handful of children and to give them a meaningful future. It is still there today, still being used as a family home for needy children, and is set in a picture postcard panorama that surely cannot fail to inspire any child or visitor towards the promise of a better tomorrow.

Imst was the beginning of Gmeiner's dream and the start of his concept which has grown in a little over half a century into one of the world's most significant child welfare organisations, active in 131 countries and with facilities including schools, youth programmes and training and medical centres, in addition to the "family" of over 400 villages.

A simple plaque on the wall of the first Imst house reads: "It is easy to do good - if many people help."

Inside the garden a permanent memorial reminds us that the founder, who died aged 67 in 1986 from cancer, was a peace-loving man who wanted only to see all children in need, whatever their creed or colour or race, to be given the prospect of a more secure future.

And while the idea of his villages for orphans began to blossom in Europe in the aftermath of war, he then took the concept to Asia and a highly-successful fund-raising campaign established further villages there after the Korean War in the 1950s.

Others have followed in regions of more recent conflict like the Palestinian Territories, Kosovo and West Africa, but for those like Richard Pichler who are now carrying the organisation forward, there is also a wider challenge to face.

In western Europe, for example, there may not be many orphans of war, but there is an increasing direction by governments, especially those under financial pressure, to off-load their state childcare responsibilities to groups in the private or charity sectors like SOS Children's Villages.

The result is that many of their villages outside conflict zones now take in children sent to them under court authority orders because their parents may be in prison or have histories of violence or serious drug dependence which rule them out of safe parentage. Equally, the villages look after children who, because of parental sickness, poverty or neglect, can no longer remain at home.

It is a double-edged problem for the childcare agencies because the directors of the national SOS Children's Villages operations we have talked to say the number of these children in need is growing rapidly at a time when many governments want to cut back on their commitments.

The quinquennial SOS Children's Villages general assembly, which brings together representatives of the organisation from across the world and which sets future policy, was due to discuss these issues in Innsbruck just after we left.

Within their overall aim of becoming a global leader in the long-term, family-based care of children, the assembly agreed strategic objectives until 2008. These included increasing the number of children in their care by 50 per cent, providing special help for the children of families affected by AIDS, and a fund-raising programme to boost the organisation's revenues by half.

As this vision was unfolding, we continued with two shortish hops to Vienna and Budapest, before beginning the longest leg so far – a run of 1,500 km or so down to Athens.

It is as if our little Greek Goddess knows she is heading for home. The air conditioning system which fried us all the way to Rome and back has been fixed (an electrical problem, says the engineer in Vienna) and the Kid and I are in good heart.

At our fairly leisurely pace it will take us four days to get to Athens with a one-night stop in Belgrade, another in Skopje and a third somewhere round Thessaloniki. And the first sign we notice that times are getting tougher, economically-speaking, is the state of the roads.

They have been worsening since we left Vienna which, although it would claim to belong more to the west than to the east of Europe, is probably where the dividing line begins. They have deteriorated further as we exit Budapest, and become worse still as we approach Belgrade.

We are travelling down what our map tells us is virtually the one and only motorway in Serbia-Montenegro. In fact, to call it a motorway at all is a triumph of hope over experience, of spin over substance.

Downhill skiers would call it a slalom.

Before the United Nations lost patience and took the highly un-UN step of shooting real bullets at people to stop the recent war between Serbs and Croats, my guess is that nearly everyone's tanks had used this road on manoeuvres. The result is a set of ruts running so deep down the lanes that when poor little GG gets into them she might as well be a tram.

"Don't see much point in hanging onto the wheel," said the Kid in an understandable huff. "I'll take a kip and she can steer herself."

But come to think of it, there's an even clearer way of assessing the local roads to tell when a nation's economy is on a downer: it's a game called "see how many ways we can relieve our visitors of their spending money" and these are the rules:

- *Rule No 1:* Declare that your country has nothing whatever to do with Europe (unless it suits you of course – like entering the Eurovision Song Contest) so that agreements like Green Card car insurance can be declared not applicable.
  Result: Throw 80 euros (oh yes, that will do nicely) into the pot or go to jail.

- *Rule No 2:* Park your police car behind a bush, jump out when the first car comes along, wave something that looks suspiciously like a torch at it and claim it has been exceeding the speed limit.
  Result: Throw 20 euros (or however much you have on your person) into this pocket please, or go to jail.
  Note: this trick can be repeated as often as reasonably possible; three times in five miles for example.

- *Rule No 3:* Erect dog-race starting traps across the highway at strategically-placed intervals (guideline: one every two miles) and charge motorists a toll fee every time they pass Go.
  Result: Throw 10 euros into the pot or go to jail.

By the time we reach Belgrade we have a lot less money and a lot more of an idea why they need it more than us as we sign into the Jugoslavija Hotel, once one of the great hotels of Europe, but which now stands, all 800 rooms of it, battle-scared, bomb and fire-damaged, on the banks of the Danube.

Next we come to Macedonia, which is beautifully formed from parts of the former Yugoslavia, where we discover they play another version of the Serbian game with the same first two rules (except the stakes are smaller) while No 3 insists that tolls are collected even before the road gets made up to a proper standard.

It's an ingenious payment-in-advance system for the benefit of future motorists and one that we have not come across before.

Not surprisingly, after two days of bumping and barging her way through all of this, little GG is finding the strain a bit much.

More electronic problems have surfaced – this time with one of the fuel tank gauges, whose needle falls limply back to zero even though we know we filled the tank up to its maximum capacity only 100 km ago (unless, oh surely not, we've sprung a leak from the tank somewhere) – and there's a small problem with the exhaust.

Still, as we enter Greece and she purrs sensuously along the higher standard of road, the Kid and I decide on a treat: we will take her up to Litichoro beside Mount Olympus, home of the 12 Greek Gods, to make her feel at home. It's not much of a distance from there to Athens where we can put her on a ferry across to Turkey and she can rest and relax.

There's some good news too from the commander back at base: "Huge publicity all over the place and a total of £21,000 raised for SOS Children's Villages from our efforts so far," he says in an excited email message.

Oh, and the Kid finds a report on the Internet from China that the World Health Organisation has at last declared the country open to foreign visitors again after a decline in the toll of the SARS epidemic which has now claimed more than 900 lives and put over 9,000 people in hospital.

Perhaps it means we can try again for our preferred Route One through China - rather than going north through Mongolia and Russia or south through Asia.

But for the moment we will just take a breather with GG on Mount Olympus, in the lap of the gods.

Distance driven so far: 5,700km

Chapter 12
A MINOR INDISCRETION

WEEK FOUR: Mr Papalikis, genial director of the SOS Children's Village on the outskirts of Athens, is looking rather flustered.

We had been late rising, and with the press conference due to begin in only an hour, the jovial "Papa", as we had come to know him, had come to the door to ask if he could move the car up the hill to a spot where the photographers would have a good shot of her and the kids.

But oh dear, Papa's ever-present smile seemed to have gone missing.

"It was only 30 metres. Very honest. I did nothing wrong to make her …"

"Do what?" ask the Kid and I in unison.

"Well she …" Papa's English is broken at the best of times, but now it has disintegrated. He flourishes his hands downwards and outwards like the conductor of an orchestra. "She just …whoosh."

The three of us go up the hill in a hurry.

Papa's whoosh is there for all to see – a patch of gasoline which glistens in the morning sun and is, even as we stand and gawp, transforming itself from a puddle into a pool across the tarmac under the skirts of our embarrassed Goddess. It looks just like she has wet herself.

Thinking back, I suppose we should have warned Papa that the fuel gauges had been playing up; should have explained that we had already arranged for an engineer to take a look at her as soon as the press conference was over. But there hadn't been time. We had just handed him the keys and rushed off to get dressed.

But now what? It wasn't Papa's fault; wasn't anybody's really. Not even GG's, we supposed, although she certainly had not picked the best of times to relieve herself of fuel.

As far as we knew she had never done it before and the reasons why it had happened now would have to wait for the engineer to determine later, but just at the moment there was a significant problem.

The pool is large; the sun is hot. "We'll have to move her straight away and get something over this," I said in a panic. "We can't let the

73

children near her and neither, oh heavens, can we let the journalists see what's happencd – just imagine what they'll have to say about it!"

Papa is getting the drift. "Newspaper and TV people here 30 minutes," he says, "we move car quick. Yes?"

And we do; pretty darned quick.

There is no way that we can start her up of course – one spark with all this fuel around and there would surely have been a spectacular end to our summer. So, slowly and oh so gently, I just slip the handbrake off and allow GG to roll 50 or so metres back down the hill to a spot where, OK, the media's pictures won't be so good and the open-air reception will be missing its star, but at least there's a chance that her indiscretion can stay a secret.

The journalists arrive. In fact, with the Goddess's Greek connections and the already well-publicised story of our journey, we find that the media corps from the motoring press in Athens turns up in droves.

There are also several executives from the local dealer organisation which is representing GG's owners and our corporate sponsors at this event. They have come, not unnaturally, armed to the teeth with speeches extolling the benefits and performance of the car.

Equally naturally, I find they now need to have a quiet word with me before the action starts and I notice that several of their more senior members of staff are being dispatched to GG's hiding place around the corner to see what can be done.

For me, a trained journalist who will be forever a follower of fire engines, what happened next does not give me the greatest pride.

I think I have come to justify it by reasoning that I needed to save GG from a public humiliation.

At any rate, with Athens' finest motoring newshounds now all assembled at the lavish reception, I then embark on one of the longest presentations they have probably ever suffered with the dual purpose of (a) allowing enough time for the sponsor's cohorts to set about hiding all traces of GG's unfortunate sins, and (b) of wearying the audience under the hot sun, to such an extent that they would consider the need for a cooling glass of wine infinitely preferable to the admittedly shortish walk around the corner to where GG is resting, powerless and in shame.

And it worked.

Forgiving myself for not delivering the star attraction into their midst, I am also thankfully able to explain that since so many of them have clogged up the driveway by arriving in large and expensive cars of their own, I have not actually been able to get the Goddess close to the reception area and they will have to walk, if they really want to, to see her in person.

Few of them do. And actually, by the time they have had a few glasses of our host's very fine wine, no-one seems really bothered that I should start her up, or to question why the sprinkling of sand under her body should be anything other than a very sensible safety precaution, or even to ask me questions about her fuel consumption which I might, in the present circumstances, find rather difficult to answer.

Papa comes over when they have all gone. He is laughing again."That was close shaving, no?" he says. Close shaving it certainly was. Local Daewoo engineers later diagnosed that a faulty valve between the Goddess's two fuel tanks had caused the fuel loss and said they had fixed the problem, but if we had been going along somewhere when the leak had sprung, goodness knows what might have happened.

Two days later and we are about to leave Athens on a ferry across the Aegean from the port of Piraeus bound for the island of Chios, and there to catch another boat to the mainland of Turkey as our journey continues. According to our new-found friends in Greece we are about to leave civilization.

Piraeus is one of the most ancient ports in the world. It is set in a perfect natural harbour, and it was from here that many of the Greek explorers and traders set out thousands of years before modern history began to lay the foundations of one of the greatest empires the world has ever known.

The characters and consignments may have changed, but today I imagine that the scene at Departure Dock H is much as it would have been for centuries.

In the usual way of things in this part of the world, nothing much happens until a deadline draws near. It is that way too at Piraeus as, until two hours before its daily departure, the ticket office taking bookings for Nel Line's ferryboat *Mytilene* is closed and the dockside beside it is deserted.

Then, as if from nowhere, the world descends. Long lines of cars, dozens of lorries and the best part of a thousand people materialise from every direction, together with their bags, baggage and pet dogs, and an entourage of motorbikes, scooters and bicycles. On this day, as it happens, there are also around 100 soldiers from the Greek army being sent on a training assignment to one of the islands.

Responsibility for making sure it all happens by sailing time is someone whose official position I do not know, but whose function I would describe as similar to the ringmaster in a circus.

He is a large man, built in the Pavarotti mould and wearing loosely-fitting khaki-coloured clothes. He directs vehicles onto the ship with a combination of elaborate hand signals, orders barked through drivers' windows, and by sharp whistle blasts which he uses as a substitute for words for those foreign people like us who don't understand his language.

It is obvious that he enjoys the performance.

Several of the ship's company, dressed smartly in all-white uniforms, are sent to flit around him with minor tasks. He doesn't bother with the walk-on passengers who file in through the various entranceways, but takes charge instead of loading the full complement of vehicles, big and small, striding out to meet them in the queue and then walking them into the stomach of the ship with his bark-and-whistle combination.

As the time for sailing draws near and his exhortations more determined, sweat turns the colour of his clothing several shades darker from shoulder to toe.

The Kid and I watch spellbound as we wait in the queue.

Big lorries go in before cars. A driver, with the beard of a pirate, stripped to the waist and wearing a cloth as a headdress against the heat of the cab, is bustled and bullied by the whistling Pavarotti until he has inched his huge load into a niche below deck.

There is the hubbub of a crowd all around. Girls tearfully wishing their soldiers goodbye; excited families going on holiday; a mother who screams in vain as her daughter turns her back on the mainland to seek a new life.

Just then there is a knock on our window and a man with an evil grin is pointing for us to look underneath the car.

"Oh no, it can't be," I say to the Kid as we jump out in horror.

We stare at the pool on the ground. Already I can feel that same sick feeling of the press conference welling in my stomach.

"Surely to God she can't have peed herself again," the Kid exclaims. The crowd senses another drama and starts to gather round. I sneak a look in Pavarotti's direction. He doesn't miss much. Like every good ringmaster he has a nose for trouble. There's a shrill blast of his whistle and he's pointing for us to take the car and move it to one side, away from the next intake.

He has already shepherded all the lorries on board and most of the cars.

"Oh no, you can't do this, not now," I say to anyone, but especially to GG. And I cry out to warn the Kid: "He's spotted that we're leaking fuel and he's not going to let us on."

We have a huddle.

"Is it coming out now?" We take a quick look underneath. No, nothing dripping.

"Right, then I reckon we've got a choice of two," I say. "Either we can own up that we've got a problem or we can move the car forward and make out that it's come from someone else's."

I look at my watch. Just 15 minutes left.

"There's not much time. Which way do you vote?"

The Kid doesn't take long. And anyway, I think I knew his answer already. "Let's go for it," he says, and with that he's in the car and starting her up.

I walk over to Pavarotti as nonchalantly as I can. "Problem?"

"No, no problem," he says, "your car too high (he points to GG's rooftop "bonnet" where we keep our clothes luggage) I put you where more space. OK?"

"Yes, yes. OK," I said with much relief. And there's a spring in my step as I go to take the news back through the crowd to Karaoke.

"Terribly sorry, hope I didn't give you a fright old bean." It's the man with the devilish grin, who now turns out to have a voice with an awfully English accent.

"That stuff under your car – it's just run-off water from the air-conditioning unit. All cars do it, you know, even Rolls-Royces. Mixed with a bit of fuel lying on the dockside ... I suppose you thought you had a fuel leak." He begins to haw-haw like the jackass he is.

Never before had I felt so much like punching someone - but let's just say that maybe it was because GG, a lady, was present that I decided to ignore him.

"Oh, you'll never know how unfunny you are," I said.

Was Greece the end of civilization? We'll have to see. But for the remainder of the week we spend three days driving more than 1,500 km across the mostly flat and sparsely populated plains of central Turkey in an effort to make up some lost time. GG gives us no further problems and, in fact, seems to be refreshed from her rest on two ferryboat journeys across from Greece. The outside temperature is mostly around 40C but we treat her gently, as the base commander advises, with regular stops to cool her down.

Distance driven so far: 8,000km

Chapter 13
CROSSROADS

WEEK FIVE: Week five brings us to a major crossroads in our plans.

After a solid spell of driving across Georgia and Azerbaijan we reach the Black Sea port of Baku and a pre-arranged haven at the SOS Children's Village. The roads, for the most part across these two former Soviet-bloc countries, have been rutted and often pot-holed, but little GG's suspension has stood up to the test remarkably well.

At several points we have come to bless the wisdom of Yves Fourdin in fitting bull-bars to her front when various livestock, ranging from stray dogs to herds of homeward-bound cattle, have barred our way. The fuel gauges have once more reverted to inaccuracy, and there is an uneasy presence in our minds – thankfully not so far realised – that GG might pee herself again. But we escape our closest call to running out of fuel by waking the attendant at a remote garage of hand-cranked pumps in rural Georgia and siphoning in their fuel of unknown octane through the girls' stockings which Snapper had been given in Paris.

The turning point to our plans, when it arrives, is not unexpected - but disappointing nonetheless. Despite an official all-clear of the SARS epidemic in China, we hear from our sponsors' contacts in Shanghai that the authorities are still unwilling to reduce their astronomic (and unacceptable) escort fee of US$ 25,000. No only that, but the chaotic state of the country's administration could mean a delay of several weeks before the papers eventually arrive.

There is a double blow too, when we hear from our charity partners that a Russian entry visa – the key to our Route 2 option of turning north – is now similarly timed-out as the result of a recent reorganisation of that country's immigration systems.

"So that's it then," I say to the Kid when we catch up with email news on our first night at Baku, "now there is really only one option left – Route 3. We'll have to go round China to the south and just hope there is a boat to get us across the finishing line on the last leg up from Vietnam."

Which Way Next?

It has been a gruelling last few days. Since leaving the UK on June 9 the Kid and I have driven 9,000 km at an average of around 250 km each day. But the truth is that in the first period when we were flitting about Europe the mileage was not so great, which has had the consequence that recently we have been travelling much further than the daily average – and spending a lot more time in the car.

The format too has changed, as our initial programme of twice-a-week dates with the media circus arranged by our sponsors at some of the most sophisticated cities in the West, has now given way to less frequent and less glamorous stopovers at the sites of some of the children's villages.

Out of the spotlight and in the car there is no escaping one another.

I always knew it would be this way from when I asked the Kid if he would join me on the trip. Travelling together for several months confined in a space not much bigger than a bath was never going to be easy. For the first few days, with Snapper on board, there was always the comfort, if we needed it, of another person to deflect our emotions. But now he is gone and there are just the two of us.

"Well, what do you think of it so far?" I asked the Kid one morning as we set off on another day's driving towards a distant destination.

"Great," he says.

"Oh that's OK then," I venture, and add, prompting for more: "are you glad you came?"

"Yeah, yeah," he says, "it's great."

Which is how you may gather that flowing conversation has not been the greatest highlight of this journey so far.

But to take that as a problem of major consequence would be quite unfair. I had better say more.

We are an odd couple, the Kid and I. Often, probably to the chagrin of both of us, we are taken to be father and son. But while it is true that in looks I could indeed be mistaken for his dad, neither one of us has come to see it that way.

"Him? My dad? Piss off," says the Kid in that eloquent style of his to an inquiring petrol pump attendant somewhere in Macedonia who fortunately does not have the greatest command of English. "Thanks, but I'm very happy with the one I've got."

By another happy coincidence, with him being on the high side of 6ft 3ins (1.87m), and me on the low side of 5ft 10ins (1.75m), and with a number of other distinguishing features about our anatomy which are certainly too personal to mention, I can also be sure that both of us think that only a fool could seriously entertain any father-and-son connection for long.

But the likes and un-likes we share go much further than that.

Beer, sport, sporty ladies and a love of adventurous travel are perhaps not the normal pursuits of a 54-year-old, but they happen to be a good fit for the Kid, just turned 26, from Liverpool.

So that's all right then.

And even if conversation has been a little on the thin side here and there we get along fine.

The truth of it is that as I had met the Kid, who is the third son of a teacher mum and a retired headmaster, only a few months before, a lot of what we are both discovering about each other's personalities is happening simply while we drive along.

"Sometimes I think all of this is a bit like reality-TV with the pair of us being thrown together with everyone watching to see what happens," says the Kid in one of his more communicative moments.

I tell him I know just what he means.

Thankfully, although it is undoubtedly a fact that neither of us – or probably anyone else for that matter - foresaw the size and scope of this adventure before it began, we both seem to have sufficiently different but complementary skills to see it through.

I'll give some examples to explain the idea.

When we are in for an all-day driving session we share the burden: one hour on, one hour off. It's a more-than-sensible division of labour, we both agree. But while the theory is perfect, the practise is not – since it turns out that neither of us is much good at being the other's passenger.

Here's a for instance: "For goodness sake slow down, we've got half the world to get across yet," I find myself saying, while the kid's favourite counter is: "If you don't let the thing get out of third gear soon the rev-counter will shoot off the dial."

But somehow we still get along fine.

And here's another similarity where the differences end: the Kid is a university graduate while I left school at 16. In fact, he's more than a graduate; as I mentioned earlier, he has a masters degree in electronics which means he can work all the communications things we need like laptop computers and bluetooth connections, and fix up PowerPoint displays and tap into a hotel's phone system when we need to get our messages on the internet. And I can't.

But then again, he's no good at standing up in front of audiences and telling them about our adventures or why they should put their hands in their pockets and give generously to the organisation looking after the welfare of some of the world's most unfortunate and deserving children.

But somehow we get along fine.

Perhaps the thing that holds us together most is the single-minded determination we share to succeed by reaching South Korea in the little Greek Goddess.

Now that we've heard the disappointing news about the demise of our alternative Route Plans 1 and 2, there is work to be done in getting past the crossroads at Baku and setting up a new itinerary to get us round the south of China.

We consult our maps and charts.

Going south is no easy matter. It's that frustrating political circus again. Iran hasn't liked the Americans (and they unfortunately appear to consider the British as one and the same) since President Bush accused them of helping neighbours Iraq in the recent war and put them on his "Axis of Evil" list. Pakistan and India have one of the world's longest-running arguments over Kashmir and the northern territories, Bangladesh is said to be full of bandits, and Burma (now Myanmar) has terrorist troubles.

The Kid and I sit down to do some serious talking or, to put it more accurately, we ask Ugur Zeynally, who is our host at the Baku children's village and who knows more about what is really going on in this part of the world than we will ever sniff at, what we need to do.

He doesn't waste words. "If you can get yourselves entry visas for Iran, Pakistan and India then it will be worth setting off again – but otherwise, you might as well just call it a day, turn the car around and head back home."

No-one had said anything like that to us before.

"Right then," said the Kid, summing up the situation in his usual way. "That's great."

Pakistan was the first to provide a permit. No problem with getting into their country, said the helpful official at their functional little embassy building in Baku. And we were lucky too because the border to the north where we would exit into India had been opened again only in the last couple of days. He listened to our story about fund-raising for children and said they would waive the usual two-weeks-to-wait rule.

"Right then," said the Kid. "That's great."

Iran was next. I could have sworn the man at the desk said his name was Mr Canbecivil, but I may have been wrong.

In fact, things weren't very civil for us right from the start.

"Mr Blair and Mr Bush best friends," said Mr Can-be-civil, noting that I came from England, but presumably confusing this with the north-east American state with an approximately similar name.

And it didn't get better.

"I see you are a writer – writers are journalists, yes? Papers tell lies about us. Iran doesn't like writers."

I get the drift.

Mr Can-be-civil is sounding distinctly like this is not going to be one of those occasions when he lives up to his name.

We don't even get as far as pleading the humanitarian case.

"This will be problem application. I will send off to Teheran but could take two weeks for answer, maybe three …," Mr Canbecivil shrugs his shoulders in a gesture which didn't need Einstein to interpret.

"Right you are then. Great," said the Kid, who had been listening over my shoulder.

We went outside. "If we can't get through Iran from here that means going the long way round to Pakistan through Afghanistan," I said.

Ugur had already talked about this option to me. "They give visas, but the place is still bloody dangerous," he warned.

"OK then," said the Kid, "so far we've won one and lost one. Let's try India. If they say yes, I'm up for giving Afghanistan a go."

"And if they don't …" I start to question.

But that was as far as it went. The Kid's communication skills had evidently been stretched more than enough already.

We find the Indian embassy in one of the more distant suburbs from Baku city centre. It is a pleasant enough building, nearer in age to two centuries than one, I should think, and with some nice features like ornate fireplaces, handsome mirrors and wooden floors with crafted inlays. Today, unfortunately, most of the ground floor is hidden under a collection of large dust sheets.

"I'm so sorry," says a chirpy voice from under the covers. "You will have to excuse the mess but we have the decorators in." An Indian official, with twinkling eyes and a bustling friendliness, emerges from somewhere to greet the Kid and me.

We explain our story: Our marathon journey – raising money for children – needing to change plans – can we have a visa please, it's rather urgent.

Mr Chirpy Voice listens intently. "It's all a bit irregular," he says, "these things normally take a couple of weeks you know?"

We say we do know, but would the ambassador kindly consider this as an urgent request in all the circumstances because we are on a schedule to complete the journey in 80 days and SOS does have more children's villages in his country than any other place in the world, and by the way did he know that the British now have more of their restaurants than anyone else's and it's a fact that there's a store on virtually every street corner run by one of his fellow countrymen which stays open until 10 o'clock every night even on Sundays?

The official withers under the onslaught.

"Just one minute," he says chirpily, picking up the phone and jabbering animatedly into it for what seemed like an age.

Now he puts it down. "Please come back in half an hour. The ambassador will see you then."

We are back on the dot of 30 minutes. Some of the larger dust sheets have been taken away. Mr Chirpy Voice is leading us upstairs and introducing us to the ambassador, an older man with spectacles and a similarly genial manner, who would like us to sit with him sharing tea and biscuits while we explain again why we would so urgently like him to issue us with an entry visa to his wonderful country.

We do as he says. Or, to be more precise, I do as he says while the Kid takes it all in and just adds the odd 'great' when the occasion allows. "My name is J .S. Pande," explains the ambassador, "although most people call me JP. Now as it happens you might just be in luck. I have had a lifetime's interest in motor cars and I like nothing better than driving them long distances."

We had our visa in no time at all. JP had already done the groundwork. After a while there was a small interruption to our teatime smalltalk as Mr Chirpy Voice knocked on the door and told him the message he was waiting for had come through from someone high up in Delhi.

"There you are," said JP brandishing a slip of paper, "I've got you a special clearance."

So, with two of our three new visas now in hand, we reckoned it was worth setting off from Azerbaijan on the next stage across the Caspian Sea and into Kazakhstan. Route Plan 3, taking us round the south of China, had become a viable prospect after all. It would mean negotiating our way through the dangers of Afghanistan and Myanmar, and we still needed to confirm that a ferryboat service would be available to get us to South Korea from Vietnam. But after our period of greatest despair so far, a way forward from the crossroads at Baku had opened up.

We had reached the point where our journey would become a true adventure.

Distance driven so far: 9,000 km

Chapter 14
COMING OF AGE

WEEK SIX: We are looking forward to fulfilling what will now be the last stopover visit of our original route. At Tashkent, far to the east of Uzbekistan, we plan to pick up an entry visa for Afghanistan and then turn south, away from China, under the new Plan 3.

Uzbekistan is of course another of the now-independent states of the old Soviet Union, struggling to find its way in a brave new world. There we will travel along more of the ancient Silk Road including a visit to Samarkand with its rich history as the mystical bazaar where the tough fur traders came down from Russia to meet camel trains loaded with rugs and carpets arriving from the south and the Chinese and Asians coming in from the east with their silks and spices.

The journey of more than 2,000 km from Baku across the Caspian Sea to Kazakhstan and then through Uzbekistan was never going to be easy in a family hatchback car … but little did we realise it would turn out to be quite so gruelling.

The Caspian Sea is the biggest lake in the world. Unlike the Mediterranean and its near neighbour the Black Sea, it has no connection with any ocean and therefore cannot really be called a sea and I can only suppose the mapmakers thought it deserved that classification because of its size. It is, in fact, rather larger than the whole of mainland UK.

It is bordered by no fewer than five countries – Azerbaijan, Kazakhstan, Russia, Turkmenistan and Iran – and anyone with a lake-faring nature might therefore expect it to be as busy as heck with ships of all shapes and sizes plying their way to and fro' between the nations with passengers and cargo.

But not a bit of it. The truth, as far as we could tell, is that there is just one ferryboat in operation.

The good ship *Azerbaycan* is an 11,485-ton rust-bucket, built by the Russians more than 20 years ago. She sails on a regular basis from Baku in Azerbaijan to Turkmenistan carrying an assortment of cargoes but no foreign passengers - because President Turkman, as we have already discovered, is a capricious dictator at the best of times and very particular about who he will allow into his country.

Other than that, for people like us who don't want to drive a prodigious distance all the way round the lake, there is only the *Azerbaycan's* secondary route from Baku to the port of Aqtau in Kazakhstan – and she sails in that direction only when she wants to.

Again, as far as we can make out, the decision about whether or not to cast her off is made by a pot-bellied shipping manager who sits with his assistant on most days in a small office at the Baku dockside playing cards to pass the time while alternatively eating grapes and smoking cigarettes in equal measure. We know this because, like scores of would-be passengers throughout the city, we make a daily call or visit to his offices, to find out whether he has made up his mind that she can leave that day for Aqtau.

The determining factor, it seems, is money. When enough cargo has arrived at the dock – either on trucks or by trainloads which can be shunted straight into the ship – and he is satisfied that enough people have called or visited his office to make it worth his while, the word is passed that the ship will sail.

We have waited three days for pot-belly's decision; others have waited a week.

But now is the hour. Ugur, the dynamic and well-connected director of our hosting SOS Children's Village, gets the magic phone call and we, like the 50 or so other passengers waiting all over town, now descend on the quayside at Baku as if a siren has sounded, to claim our place on the Russian rust-bucket.

The journey is scheduled to take 18 hours, with the first eight lasting through the night. Being a lake and with the weather in the haze of high summer, the water is a lifeless calm. Our accommodation, if that is the right word for it, is a cubbyhole of a cabin with two sets of soiled mattresses and an outside toilet which seems to be shared by most of the passengers on our deck and which smells like the open sewer it undoubtedly is.

"Oh well," says the Kid, trying to make the best of it, "I'll go to see what's cooking." He heads off to the restaurant with some Kazakh truck drivers who have hit on the brain-damagingly good idea that a vodka-drinking session might be the best way of enlivening our surroundings.

And that was how it was as the shambling *Azerbaycan*, with little GG tucked inside her between all the lorries and train containers, began to pick her way across the vastness of the Caspian towards Aqtau, leaving the pot-bellied manager back in Baku to hop in his car and bank the profits.

It seemed that one sleepless night later, and after an unexpected technicolour meal for the fish from a young English adventurer now more than a little unsteady on his feet, we would soon be back in the Goddess and on our way.

But someone had forgotten to tell Kazakhstan that we were coming.

Late into the next afternoon, as the boat billowed its way in a cloud of black diesel smoke into the outer approaches of Aqtau harbour, the throb of the engines first began to slow, and then stopped completely.

Hour after hour went by as we sat listlessly at anchor.

In the restaurant, the truck drivers had taken to playing chess with empty vodka bottles. In the toilets, the smell had reached a level where handkerchief masks were now required; anyone who has undergone the humility of a faecal fat collection in hospital will recognise the scenario. In the hold, I imagine, GG was feeling rather lonely.

More time went by.

The captain was not in the mood for giving out information. Rumours came and went: the engines wouldn't start; bailiffs wanted to seize the ship; urgent repairs were being carried out below decks. All were eminently possible, but none apparently true. Another night began to fall.

Eventually, such is the way with these kind of things, the real word started to pass around: there was another boat already in the dock – an oil tanker which would take all night to unload. The captain was sorry, he said, but there was nothing he could do.

So that was it. The *Azerbaycan*, trundling around the world's largest lake, working to its own timetable and failing to tell anyone where it was going until the very last moment, would just have to wait.

And so would we – pacing around, avoiding the soiled mattresses, avoiding the vodka, avoiding the toilets, for another long and sleepless night.

In the big break-up of the old USSR, an independent Kazakhstan emerged by size as a huge and significant country. Sliced from its Russian masters in the north, it stretches from the Caspian Sea to China across the vast plains of Central Asia in a land mass which houses fewer people per square kilometre in parts than even Canada or Australia.

For the most of it, especially in the east, the landscape is almost lunar in its makeup with flat and lifeless semi-desert leading away to grey escarpments on distant horizons. There are few towns of any size and, here and there, where communities huddle around a thicket of struggling trees, life is patently hard for those who eke out their lives in the scattering of square, white-washed, primitive buildings.

We had been warned about the state of its roads by the Kazakh truck-drivers. On the boat, pinning down our map with bottles to each corner on the restaurant table, they had marked out those that they knew would be rough and without a hard top surface - and there were many of them.

At first it seemed they had been mistaken. Asphalt of reasonable quality stretched beyond where they had scribbled their signs and the Kid and I were congratulating ourselves for taking a chance on making up lost time on the hunch that improvements might have been made, when – bang! – the road simply disappeared.

The Kid was dozing in the passenger seat trying to catch up on lost sleep.

"That's torn it," I shouted as he woke with the first jarring bump, "we've just run out of road."

GG was almost down to a walking pace. She hadn't faced anything like this before. Back in Georgia, where the roads were pot-holed and dangerous, at least we had been able to avoid the worst patches by carefully weaving a path between them. But this was different.

Here, the whole road was a problem – a surface of unmade stones, sometimes loose, sometimes not, and often rutted or pot-holed without warning. Judging by the Kazakhs' markings on our charts there would also be a stretch like this for a very long way ahead.

"Nothing else for it," said the Kid, sensing another adventure. "We'll just have to head for Beyneu like they told us."

Now Beyneu, as another mark on the map reminded us, was a place where the Kazakhs had said we might be able to get out of trouble.

The ups and downs of unmade roads didn't make much difference to their big 18-wheeler Mercedes trucks, but they had looked underneath our little Goddess and decided to give us a chance. "If you can get to Beyneu," they said, "we hear it's got a station where you can put the car onto the back of a train."

And that, we decided, as another blow to the suspension smacked our teeth together, now sounded like a darned good idea.

Actually, it wasn't Beyneu that was to be our saviour. It was a small hamlet near Beyneu called Aqzhiait.

We discovered this when we finally reached the station at Beyneu at 3am after a nightmare drive of 400 km which GG – and her suspension – somehow survived along those unmade roads.

It didn't sound far. "Just another 60 km. Get yourselves to Aqzhiait by 10am and you can put the car on the train," said a helpful policeman as we angled back the seats in GG and tried to catch a few hours respite from our third sleepless night.

We set off early. According to our map there wasn't even a road to Aqzhiait, but the policeman was certain there was and anyway, why would it have a station there if no-one could get to it?

We were soon to find out.

For those who don't know (and I would suggest that very – no, make that very, very – many people don't), the place called Aqzhiait which straddles the border of Kazakhstan and Uzbekistan has not been blessed with the best comforts of life.

It consists of a gaggle of small and dilapidated houses, a large number of dogs which roam around in a pack, a school, a factory making parts for a less glamorous sector of the oil industry, and a station which I can only assume was once busy enough to deserve its existence.

That must have been a long time ago.

There is also, rather strangely, a ramp built of mud, concrete and stones up which cars like our GG can launch themselves off into space and, if they're lucky, land on one of a series of flat-bedded rail trucks which have been left there in a siding with the hope of being hooked up to a passing train at some future time.

Even then, I can only tell you this because we managed to get GG along that 60 km of something or other to reach it.

The map was right. It wasn't a road; well, certainly not in any conventional sense.

The route from Beyneu to Aqzhiait – and it is the only one – would guarantee to test the suspension of a tractor. It is a cross between a farmer's lane and a cart-track with ruts in places two or three feet deep and a loose top surface of soil and sand.

How little GG, a car designed for ladies to drive with wind in their hair, ever made it to the end without losing a wheel or breaking an axle, or both, I shall never know. And especially since it began to rain halfway along, which quickly turned the top surface into a sticky mud pudding that clung to the tyres and caused them to lose all traction.

The Kid, who was at the wheel for most of the time, found the car sliding off towards ditches first one side and then the other, as little GG went out of control like she was skating on ice.

Every few yards I would go round the tyres and pull the mud off with my hands - only to find, of course, that another clingy mass had soon replaced it.

"Wow," said the Kid when we finally reached the station and its take-off ramp, "now I know what it must be like to go on safari."

The train, when they eventually found one willing to stop and hook itself up to our flat-level truck, took us across the border and through the jolting clackety-clack of another night while we tried to sleep inside GG, who was strapped to the top of it.

It left us at Nukus where – yes, the Kazakhs had been right again – the road we needed was in better shape, but we still faced a journey of nearly 700 km across the virtual desert between Urgench and Bukhara in central Uzbekistan.

Now here's a confession:

I find that over the last few days I have taken to talking to GG – not in a stupid way, I hope, but in the way that people might usually converse with their best friends at times like these.

Just little things like: "Hey GG, how are you today?"

91

Or, when she's done well, something of praise like: "Nice one GG, keep it going won't you?"

Or even, as she's struggled to find some speed up the steepest of hills, patting her on the dashboard and saying: "C'mon GG, you know you can do it!"

I remember once reading that talking to flowers was good for them; made them feel wanted, made them grow. And now, I guess, it's getting to me too.

Perhaps, after all, it's only natural to be unnatural.

Over the course of this trip, and the last week especially, little GG seems to have become more than just a car. I get the feeling she has come of age.

When I met her at the beginning, all decked out with her colourful decals and stripes down the side, her bonnet on top and her bull-bar of a grin, she seemed to me to have a character of her own. And now that I have come to know her better, she's shown me she can be strong as well as pretty.

The children love her. Everywhere we've been, the SOS Children's Village youngsters have had fun with her, climbed all over her, written their names in her dusty paintwork; scribbled their messages of love and goodwill to take to their friends in far-off Korea.

I find I'm in discussion with myself: "Maybe, while she's been hammering over the bumps and hollows of those terrible roads these past few days … maybe when she's felt herself sliding towards the ditch on the way to the station …"

Yes maybe, when all's said and done, she knows she would be letting everyone down if she failed to make it to the end.

Today GG is in for another test. The road to Bukhara goes through some of the most barren country we have yet encountered. Tomorrow we will reach all the fun and colour of Samarkand and Tashkent – but today there is only mile after mile of desert land punctuated by clumps of scrub grass and some thirsty trees. Outside the temperature is in the high 40s centigrade and we try to stop every hour or so to let her engine cool and give ourselves a break.

With few cars travelling either way I find myself asking GG those questions again.

"What would we do if you broke down, right out here in the desert with no-one around?"

But I needn't have worried, because this brave little car, who has already proved she can be reliable as well as everything else, simply sped through the place with hardly a murmur.

"Nice one GG," I said to her that night, "you did really well today." And I swear I saw her wire-grilled spotlights give a little flutter at the flattery.

Distance driven so far: 11,000 km

(Technical note: Engineers who checked out the car in Tashkent found she had only minor problems. The wheels needed re-tracking after their recent pounding, but another hefty jolt as we hit a pothole in the road one night had set the faulty fuel gauges working again! We have used hardly any oil.)

Chapter 15
STRANDED!

WEEKS SEVEN AND EIGHT: Last week GG came of age. Now it's been our turn.

I guess there must come a time in almost every epic journey when there is a defining moment for those taking part – a time when, quite literally, the fate of the adventure hangs in the balance.

In our case it wasn't exhaustion or sickness or those kinds of things that threatened to force us to abandon our goal; nor even that GG, who is hardly suited for the trip (or so we thought!) should give up the ghost.

No, the defining moment which all but brought an end to this hair-brained scheme for the Kid and I arrived in the rugged mountains and sandswept passes of northern Afghanistan…

The young officer at the border patrol post is apologetic. He has checked our passports, made two calls on the field telephone to his superiors, listened to our story about having driven here halfway across the world, but he is sorry: we don't have any special papers. SOS Children's Villages, the children's charity we represent, is not on his approved list and there is no way he can let us in.

It is very early in the morning. We have driven all yesterday and right through the night to reach this crossing at Termez on the northern Afghan border. But now he is telling us we must go back into the flat and dusty fields of Uzbekistan to see for ourselves what can be done.

Across the border, patrolled by soldiers like him in combat dress with machine guns, and on the other side of the high wire fence and the strip of ploughed-up 'dead man's land', lies a country which for the last 25 years has been one of the most troubled nations on earth.

We have already driven 12,000 km across 17 countries. Now we need only to pass through 650 km of Afghanistan to reach Pakistan and the south east Asian corridor along which we plan to reach our destination of South Korea by the new Route 3.

We have looked at the map and made our calculations. Afghanistan doesn't seem large. But then again, I imagine that has been the mistake that would-be invaders have been making down the centuries and, more especially, the Russians and Americans of more recent times.

Anyway, the officer is sorry. "It's dangerous in there," he says. "Only people with special permission can go in – and you don't have any."

We are evidently not the first to be turned away. He pushes a piece of paper with a typed address in my direction. It's the name of a United Nations compound about 6 km up the road.

"I suggest you go and talk to them," he says.

The Kid looks shattered. It's been a long and weary night and he has done much of the driving along winding, unlit roads to get here. "I can't believe it," he curses. "All this way, just to be told we can't get in."

We find the UN's enclave without much trouble. It is a well-known place. They set it up soon after the long lines of Afghan women and children, struggling with their meagre possessions, came flooding across the border when the Russian troops with their tanks and guns, came muscling into their country 20-odd years ago, and they expanded its importance when the Americans arrived, carpet-bombing the mountain villages and sending thousands of their men on a fruitless search for Osama bin Laden and his Al Kaeda followers in the aftermath of the 9/11 attacks in the USA.

Afghanistan has been a battleground for centuries. Its strategic importance as a crossing point between north and south, and east and west, is a prize which men have been asked to fight and die for right through history. But there's never been anything like the scenes of these last few years when millions of Afghans have fled their country under the onslaught of the armies of the super-powers.

Paradoxically, such is the topsy-turvy world in which we live, the scale of the refugee problem has led to a greater demand for those whose role it is to provide assistance in all this man-made suffering. The plight of the refugees has to be monitored and co-ordinated, and at Termez, which is the oldest UN compound of its type, all the major relief agencies are represented.

"It's dangerous in there," repeats Anwar Kholbaev, the amiable and very capable head of the UN's office for co-ordinating humanitarian affairs, when we get to see him and explain our story.

"Right now, the only people being allowed into Afghanistan are those on *bona fide* humanitarian work linked with the UN, and I'm afraid," he can hardly suppress a little chuckle at this point, "that driving a family hatchback into the place on a scattered-brained adventure – no matter how worthy the cause – doesn't qualify on any account."

The Kid and I are shell-shocked.

"But SOS does great work for refugees – including Afghans," I protested (having looked it up swiftly in my pack of reference papers). "And hey, look, if you're worried about any comeback we'll sign something saying we are doing it of our free will and…" (I have not checked with the Kid before saying this, although I felt sure he would agree).

But this was an issue on which Anwar, the UN's top humanitarian, would not be moved.

And now there was another reason. A very big reason.

We had taken Anwar out to see little GG thinking that maybe, just maybe, her seductive allure, plus the scribbled messages of innocent children's love and affection all over her paintwork, might loosen his resolve. But it was not to be.

He looked at her small tyres, confirmed with one question that she did not have four-wheel drive, and then told us: "The fact is, even if I wanted to give you permission you would never get through. The road between here and Kabul has been blocked by sandstorms for days and there have been a couple of tunnel roof-falls, which are proving hard to clear. Only the big 4x4s are getting through – and even they are having a tough time of it."

The Kid and I tried to take it on the chin.

We had rehearsed a line once or twice before on this great escapade, but now I found myself saying it for real: "One impossibility is bad enough, but two makes it really difficult."

In the language of never-say-die adventuring, that's about as close as it gets to giving up.

Next morning, unable to sleep, I was sitting on the steps of the compound entrance watching the first rays of sun reminding the world that life does go on, when I heard the drone of an aircraft. It wasn't far away. In fact, as I stood to find a better view over the fence, and despite its camouflaged colours, I could clearly make out the darkly-mottled shape of a bulky transport plane as it rose into the lightening sky and made its way lazily into the distance.

Even as I watched it go, a thought was settling in my head.

So far, on this amazing journey of ours, we have twice loaded GG onto boats (the ferries from Greece to Turkey and then across the Caspian) and once, last week, onto a train.

I took a last look at the disappearing plane. "M'm, I wonder..." I muttered.

"Colonel Hoppe will see you now. But I must warn you that he only has five minutes before he has to leave for an appointment," said the sergeant who escorted us through the sentry post at the barracks of the German Air Unit at Termez's small airfield sometime later in the morning.

Anwar, the UN's man, had given us his phone number. "I shouldn't do this," he told the Kid and me. "We are not allowed to show any favours you know, but still, in all the circumstances ..."

I knew I had to get straight to the point.

"Colonel, we are British and you are German but we have come to you because we need your help."

It was an introduction which I had rehearsed on the way here. It was cheeky. It was chancey. But it worked.

The colonel gave us double the time allowed. There was even a little twinkle in his eye as he joined in the spirit of my opening remark. "Ja," he said, "we don't often help each other do we?"

Ten minutes later and I had a promise from Colonel Wolfgang Hoppe, base commander of the large attachment of German Air Corps at Termez, whose task is to ferry peace-keeping international troops down to Kabul several times a week, that he might, just might, consider putting us and GG into the hold of one of his big Hercules aircraft.

"But first I must warn you that there will be several hurdles to overcome," he said. "We will only be able to do it if you can get permission from my High Command in Germany, we can only do it if there is a plane available with sufficient space on board, and we shall need some proof that you are on the humanitarian mission which you say."

I hardly had time to thank him before he added another condition: "Oh," he said, "and you will have to make sure you have all the right customs clearance papers for the car."

Back at the UN base Anwar listened to our story. Maybe GG had worked some magic on him too.

"No, I've never heard of it being done from here before but let's see what I can do to help," he said.

We had answers to the Colonel's requests within 48 hours.

A call to the German attaché at the embassy in Tashkent produced a faxed permission to the Air Base from Potsdam in no time at all. It was signed by someone with a very impressive rank and the Colonel read it out to us, word for word and with great delight, when we saw him next.

There was also a full set of faxed endorsements of our fund-raising mission from the SOS organisation's high command at Innsbruck. Peter Voelker, a deputy secretary-general who we had met on our visit there just a few weeks back, called me on the phone to confirm it was on the way.

"I hope you know what you're doing," he joked, but then added in all seriousness: "Afghanistan is very volatile. You don't have to do this for us you know. I have to point out that it must be your decision."

"I know," I said. "Thank you for the warning, but yes, we want to go."

Anwar, carried along by the euphoria, somehow managed to persuade his commissioner that our madcap adventure might have some benefit to the UN cause after all.

And finally we received the customs papers from an official called Illia who became so enthusiastic about the whole episode that he insisted on coming with us to meet the colonel and being chauffeur-driven there in GG.

We got the go-ahead call next day. It was the colonel's aide de camp (ADC).

"Be here tonight with the car at 17.00 hours to receive your

briefing," he said. "You will be flown by a Dutch air crew from Eindhoven under our command. There will be 'passengers' on board and we must remind you that this is a military mission. Please do not, therefore, release any information about this until the flight is over."
I put down the phone. Anwar was beaming. So was the Kid.
"It's a bloody miracle!" he said.

We reported for the flight next morning at 4.45am. After the evening briefing the Kid and I had gone out for a meal in a late-night restaurant to kill time and I had been hoping to get a few hours sleep in readiness for what I knew would be a dangerous and exciting day. But after five days of frustration and waiting around, my adrenalin was pumping as our chance approached to get going again and my brain would not slow down.
I found the Kid pacing around at 3am. It was the same for him.
"Can't sleep either?" I queried in the darkness,
"Not a chance," he said, "now I know how James Bond must feel before a mission."

At the base we drove little GG in through the gates. Rudi, the big German ADC, is standing there waiting for us. The combination of Teutonic efficiency and military planning means everything must be done on time and to the strictest regulations.
"You must park car here," he commands, directing us to an exact spot where the technicians will take over – weighing and measuring the car (although they have already done this once) checking and checking again that everything is in order before loading her into the cargo hold of the big Hercules which is standing on the far side of the runway.
I find myself patting her on the bonnet and, in that new habit of mine, passing her a goodwill wish. "Off you go GG," I say. "Not long now and we'll be on the road again."
Rudi has been assigned to us. He leads us over to the area where close on 40 soldiers are milling in the waiting area dressed in full camouflage kit. These are the "passengers" we were told about earlier. They are part of a military force, headed up by the Germans, which is trying to bring some order to Kabul.

Which Way Next?

Like us, they have been waiting around somewhere for their turn to come. But unlike us, they are not looking forward to it. Their mood is edgy. Reports on the news, even in the last few hours, have spoken of more unrest to the south of the city where Taliban forces have clashed in the hills with men loyal to the new government. Their task as peace-keepers, acting as a human shield in a civil war where only the Afghans know the difference between friends and foe, is about to test their nerve and courage to the very limit.

Rudi tries to make light of it. In real life he has a good job as an interpreter and a wife and family who he likes taking on holidays to a hotel for the over-50s in Spain. "Afghanistan is Absurdistan," he says, chuckling at his surprising line of wit. "Three months more of this and I will have done my turn to help the world. Then I will go and sit on the beach and drink some beer."

Take-off time is drawing near. The sergeant whose job is to make sure that no-one has decided peace-keeping duties in Afghanistan can do without them, takes another roll call. Then, being all present and correct, the little German army, plus me and the Kid, board a bus and trundle over the tarmac to the waiting plane.

The scene inside reminds me of one of those war films where paratroopers stand up, one after another, and hurl themselves out into space over enemy lines. Like them, we sit in two parallel rows on either side of the fuselage, but today I notice a definite lack of parachutes as one of the Dutch crew hails us with comforting words down a megaphone about what to do if we are unfortunate enough to be hit by a ground-to-air missile.

GG, enjoying her celebrity status and, looking rather pleased with herself, is strapped to the floor further down the plane where everyone can see her.

I stretch out to shake the Kid's hand as the four big engines roar us down the runway and the big bird rises into the early-morning sky.

"Put it there pal," I said. "We finally made it."

The flight didn't take much more than an hour. Inside the Hercules, with my jacket fastened to the wall, I cannot watch the world out of the window from a comfortable reclining chair like they have on conventional jets, but far, far below I imagined us crossing the border post where all of this drama began, and I thought I caught a glimpse of the roadway covered in sand and the fallen tunnel we would have found impossible to pass.

Then, suddenly, as we approach what must be one of the most dangerous airports in the world, the pilot slings the plane into a series of corkscrew manoeuvres which tip us this way and that as we hurriedly lose height in our approach towards the distant runway.

"I sink he avoids guns, ja?" says the German opposite who, until now, appeared to have been dozing peacefully since the moment we had taken off.

The Kid and I have been doing our homework these last few days.

According to the TV, more than 20 years of occupation by foreign forces have left Afghanistan a country more divided than ever.

Backed by the peace-keeping troops, a new government is struggling to restore some normality to daily life while high in the mountains, where they have proved invincible to the superpowers, pockets of Taliban and Al Kaeda forces, maybe still with bin Laden amongst them, are said to be hiding out.

In the south there have been clashes between warlords seeking to establish their fiefdoms in the vacuum left by the recent conflicts, and there is anger and resentment everywhere against the havoc wreaked on their country by the superpowers.

"The place is like a powder keg that could go off again at any time," Anwar, the UN's man at Termez had said when we asked him what our chances were.

"Think how you would feel if your country had been bombed and shelled and then bombed again for all of your life. These people are volatile, they have suffered a great deal. It doesn't take much to spark them off."

A number of foreigners had been kidnapped or shot, he added thoughtfully. "But you should be fine as long as you are careful and don't go asking for trouble."

"Well that's OK then," said the Kid when I asked if he really, really wanted to go on with our journey.

"We'll be going east from Kabul where things are relatively peaceful by all accounts and there will be fewer than 150 km to drive to the Pakistan border. We surely can't come to much harm with that?"

Which Way Next?

He made it sound easy. But he was wrong.

Not completely, as were soon to find out, but wrong just the same. We certainly could have come to harm on this never-to-be-forgotten day... and we very nearly did.

The plane ride had been all we could have wanted - a cloak-and-dagger adventure which made us feel, well yes, a bit like a pair of secret agents, and a wonderful gesture by the Dutch and Germans to help us on our way.

For a while after we landed at Kabul, reality was suspended. The manager at the airport came out to meet us personally, there were publicity pictures with the aircrew on the tarmac, our German soldier passengers marched off to keep the peace, little GG took her bow before an inquisitive new audience, and Blue Carrot (the base commander was on holiday – typical!) sent our latest story off across the airwaves from the World Media centre: 'Stranded Brits airlifted to Kabul'.

But now we were part of Afghanistan, back on the road again – and fending for ourselves in the most dangerous country of our trip.

After clearing the airport, with its rapid reminders of shellfire damage and burned-out planes, we did what we had been advised to do – we went to see if we could hook up with a convoy of "friendly" army or civilian vehicles which might be heading across to Pakistan. We asked around, but nothing we could find would be setting out for another four days.

Then we took up another suggestion and simply asked anyone and everyone to tell us what they knew about the road going east and the problems we might face.

It was a worrying catalogue: Rough and treacherous roads, undetected mines, bombed-out buildings, broken down vehicles, road blocks, car-hijackings, armed bandits ... everyone seemed to have a tale to tell.

"You can probably make it in five or six hours but set off as early as you can in case you hit trouble," was the general advice. "Whatever you do, don't still be out there after sundown."

I looked at my watch. It was just after 2pm.

"That's only about five-and-a-half hours of sunlight left. We'll be running it very close," I said to the Kid.

"Great," said my partner of few words, "let's get on with it."

The first danger point arrived all too soon. Only 10 km or so out of Kabul's damaged city, the road began to deteriorate as the thin covering of pock-marked tarmac split into patches, and then gave way completely to an unmade surface of dust, rocks and stone. Then, rising starkly against the burning sky, came the shimmering ranks of mountains, which we knew we must cross.

"My God," I said to the Kid, " this is going to be one hell of an afternoon."

I guessed the outside temperature to be up around 40 degrees.

"Gauges and dials?" I queried.

He took a quick check round the dashboard.

"Yep, everything seems fine," said the Kid. And then, in that laconic style of his, he looked up at the mountains and added: "It's a good job we filled her with fuel at the airport – there certainly won't be many garages up there."

GG was bumping along. Our brave little car, with the strengthened suspension and under-body protection installed by Yves, the engineering Walloon, had proved to us that she could take a hammering back on those tracks in Kazakhstan. But she was now playing in a different league; this was a road that had tested the soldiers of America and Russia in their tanks and armoured vehicles.

In fact, if I had actually thought about it, I would have taken a long bet that GG was the first and only family hatchback ever to have tried the journey up here.

After a while the road began to rise in the foothills and we came to a fork where I noticed that several of the trucks ahead of us were veering off.

"Aha, that's torn it," I called, "the map doesn't show any turning here. Sorry, but I haven't a clue which way we should go."

As we dithered, pulling the car to the side and preparing to take another big decision, I spotted a figure sitting just off the road on a makeshift chair in the shade of a tree. He was wearing the traditional garb and headgear of an Afghan tribesman and, too late, I noticed the rifle propped up beside him.

"Which way Pakistan?" I pointed this way and that, my voice quavering as I ventured the question.

He looked at me with my white skin and fair hair, looked at the Kid with his fresh face and boyish grin, looked at the car with her fancy decals and the bonnet on top and, quite honestly, I don't think he had ever seen anything quite like it before.

It took a moment, and then his face broke into pure devilment. "You go …" he pointed one way, "and you go fast."And with that he looked up at the sun and, making a rolling motion with his hands, left us in no doubt as to what we had to do.

"Well, what do you reckon? Friend or foe?" I asked the Kid.

"Haven't a clue," he said. And nor had I.

It was 50:50, but we agreed to take a chance and go the way he said.

The road in the mountains soon became simply terrifying; there's no other word for it. It wound around and around, often with a deep drop into oblivion off one side and with a sheer face of rock up the other. Mostly it was just wide enough for two lorries to pass, but frequently narrower than that, and the surface was deeply rutted where water had worked its way in amongst the sand and stone, and heavy loads had done the rest.

The Kid was at the wheel as we bounced and juddered along, going as fast as we dare and with his sharp eyes, as often as not, picking out the worst obstacles before we reached them. Occasionally there was another vehicle, usually a beaten-up saloon of ancient vintage that came hurtling past, or towards us, in a cloud of dust. But our problem – as with the man at the junction – was deciding whether the people inside were enemies or friends.

We remembered those warnings before we set out: how the Taliban fighters had pinned down whole convoys of trucks from hilltop positions up here as soldiers from the world's superpowers sought to invade their country. How many of them, now in the pay of volatile warlords, still roamed the mountains? We remembered the stories of car hi-jackings, of foreigners being killed and kidnapped … I thought of Terry Waite, John McCarthy, Brian

Keenan and gulped, hard.

"Don't stop for anything – or anyone," I said to the Karaoke Kid as he slowed GG to a walking pace while we worked our way around a lorry with a punctured tyre.

"But supposing we break down or we come round a corner and find the road blocked," he wondered.

"Just say some prayers and don't think about it," I said. It was years since I had prayed; I began to make up for lost time.

We had been in the mountains for a couple of hours when the car pulled alongside. It had been in the mirror, following in our dust-stream, for long enough. But now they were beside us, five of them, in an old white heap of a car, which should have been in a museum - no, make that a scrapyard - and they gestured us to stop.

There was nothing else for it. "Oh shit, now we've got trouble," I said, feeling an ache of fear inside my stomach.

"Where you go?" shouted their driver through his wound-down window.

"Peshawar … Pakistan," we both said as one.

"You hurry. Must hurry," said the driver in his best broken-down English.

"Some places," he pointed to another set of even higher mountains in the distance, "bad people. Night coming. You follow. OK?" It was the perfect set-up for a car hi-jacking. Or was it?

Our strategy plan has been to share the driving burden one hour on, one hour off these past few weeks, making the stop to stretch our legs and let the air into GG's engine as though she were a dog panting for breath. But today there is no time for such niceties. And anyway, the Kid's adrenalin is now in full flow.

"Friends or foe?" I query again as the white car pulls off in front of us and the hands in the back wave at us to follow.

"Don't know," he says, "but do we have any choice?"

The white car proves to be our saviour. For the next two hours and more we follow it through every twist and turn and across every bump and judder, picking our way through villages where the Taliban warriors still walk with Kalashnikov rifles across their backs, past the burned-out tanks and rusted debris of battles won and lost, through cavernous tunnels where we are blinded by the sand from the white car's wheels, spiralling round the mountains and ravines on our precarious ledge of a roadway.

And we stop for no-one.

In the beginning, still unsure whether they were deliberately leading us into danger, or even a trap, we hung back. But the driver coaxed us along, slowing until we had caught him up and then accelerating away when he felt sure we would follow. In turn, we grew more confident of him.

The pace quickened. It was what was needed. I know that now – because otherwise we would have been caught by the night - and he knew it too.

"Hey, this guy has been here before," I said as we mimicked our leader and veered to one side just in time to avoid a large crater, which the Kid and I would almost certainly have failed to spot.

And so it went on. Or rather, so it might have gone on if we hadn't lost ground on our leader while a lorry barred our path for an age as it ground its way slowly round an especially severe set of bends.

We found the white car slewed off the road with all five of its occupants gathered round a tyre at the back, which had blown itself apart from all the pounding.

"We have to stop now," I said to the Kid. But he had already put his foot on the brakes.

The men refused our help. I gave them the last of our water but they urged us to carry on.

"No, no - you safe. Go now," said the driver waving us away. "Mountains finish. You see."

I looked the driver full in the eyes, this man I had never met who had decided to help two fair-skinned strangers in their ridiculously conspicuous car, to survive an afternoon's lunacy in the mountains where so many of his countrymen had died.

I put my hand across my heart in the Afghan gesture of trust and friendship. "Thank you, thank you so much," I said. "I think you have probably saved our lives."

He wouldn't have understood my English, but he tilted his head in acknowledgment and I was sure he knew what I meant. And he knew just where we were too. Around the very next bend the panorama changed as abruptly as it had begun into the opening of a wide flat plain, which would take us across to Jalalabad and then on to the safety of Pakistan.

We reached the border just as the sun was dipping down for the night and just as we had hoped to do. The distance from Kabul was only 150 km, but we had taken six hours to complete the most heart-stopping journey of our lives.

Across our heads, as we arrived at the border gates, I could hear the crack of an artillery gun emplacement from the Pakistanis and the answering chatter of an Afghan machine gun as their soldiers clashed in the descending darkness of the Khyber Pass.

Poor GG, so much had happened since she took us to the airbase at Termez at 4.45 this morning, but now we were safe at last.

I put one hand on her dusty headlight. "You did fantastically well today," I found myself saying in the latest way of things.

It had been quite a day.

Distance driven so far: 12,500 km

Chapter 16
HIGHWAY TO CHAOS

WEEKS EIGHT & NINE: After running the gauntlet through Afghanistan, the door to the corridor which would lead us to the Far East was now wide open. But first there would be a drive through Pakistan and a five-day haul across the whole of India. In addition, a nasty surprise would soon arrive from Myanmar (the country formerly known as Burma).

Pakistan spoiled us for the long slog across India. Quite where their money comes from I can't be sure (except that America is known to have lately provided a great deal of what the politicians euphemistically call "financial assistance" in exchange for using their southern airbases to launch bombing forays into Afghanistan and then Iraq).

Whatever the source of the cash that built it, the world-class motorway which swept us to Lahore was a pure delight after the pounding of the Afghan mountains. GG seemed to love every minute of it, zipping along for over 500 km with only occasional stops while we took a cold drink and propped up her engine cover so she could take in some air.

It was about this time too that we became connected again to the rest of the world – or at least, we sometimes were. Let me tell you how.

We had asked for help after the Swiss mobile phone issued to us by our sponsors had exceeded its range. A package had subsequently been dispatched to us in Pakistan containing a second-hand satellite phone.

It was an impressive-looking piece of kit – a big, fat phone, two or three times the size of the largest mobile, wrapped in a leather case which added more to its bulk, and with a telescopic aerial which extended in stages to catch the signal.

But that was the problem. "This works best if you get yourself outside where there are no obstructions and you point it skywards towards a passing satellite," said the sponsors' note of instructions tucked inside.

Easier said than done

"Got cut off in mid-sentence. Bloody satellite must have gone behind the moon," said the Kid, coming in from the garden one night looking like an exasperated scuba diver. He'd just tried to call his mum.

There was no way she could call him back either – because the "periscope", as it inevitably became known, could not receive calls or, rather, no-one could seem to work out what the dialling-in code should be for this telephone *sans frontiere*.

"Upping the periscope" became our shorthand for making outgoing calls on this awesome piece of equipment, which certainly looked like the kind of thing two global adventurers ought to be using on their travels – even if we rarely completed more than a sentence or two of distant conversation.

At the border, where the rival guards of Pakistan and India strut their stuff like angry cockatoos in a show of mutual defiance, there was no sign yet of the rough and debilitating roads ahead, nor across the short leg on Day 1 to Delhi through the lush and fertile lands of the Punjab and Haryana, fed by the rivers of the emerging Himalayas.

India, Day One ...

I have written before about the contrasts and contradictions of everyday life in India, but the widening gulf between rich and poor in this nation of over a billion people is startling to the Kid.

In Delhi, the capital city and seat of government, those contrasts are never more vivid than with the green park spaces, elegant buildings and wide avenues of the central area fanning out from the spokes of India Gate and Connaught Place, being totally at odds with the narrow streets and teeming masses of the city suburbs where millions go about their daily lives scavenging an existence from refuse sacks and living in nothing short of the most abject squalor.

I had warned the Kid that he might see his first dead body here – and he didn't have long to wait: an emaciated girl of not many years lying pitifully in a bundle of rags amongst the garbage of a vegetable bazaar while the traders busied themselves nearby, readying their stalls for the next day's business.

"Looks like a gonner over there," he said in that unexcited way of his, but I could see the dart of anguish register in his eyes.

We made our way to the SOS Children's Village at Faridabad on the outskirts of the city. We needed a break from the traumas of the last few days and a chance to rebuild our energies for the long trek of 1,500 km east to Kolkata (Calcutta to you and me).

Perhaps not surprisingly, given the imbalance of wealth and poverty in this vast population, there are more SOS Children's Villages in India than anywhere else. Twenty-six SOS communities care for abandoned or destitute children in this nation of the needy, plus there are schools, colleges, training and medical facilities for the wider population; the administration is run from Faridabad, which also has a village of its own.

There is the usual welcome of wonderful, wide-eyed children agog at the stories of their visitors and instantly in love with their brave little car. But no-one is pretending that these, now less unfortunate kids, are anything but a handful from many.

"We do what we can, but it is forever just a beginning," said the village director, a jovial, mild-mannered man who was obviously doing his best.

We find some problems of our own in Delhi. Worryingly, our visa application for Myanmar, the next but one country on our new Route 3, is refused by their embassy without explanation; and I am forced to seek hospital treatment for an eye infection, which is clouding my vision. But time is important if we are to meet our deadline and we decide to push on. GG, God bless her, after her recent pounding, is checked out by a set of enthusiastic mechanics at one of our sponsors' local agents. They replace her battered shock absorbers but otherwise declare her "remarkably fit considering what you have put her through."

We are still behind schedule as we set out from Delhi and the Kid has been studying the map.

"As far as I can tell we can follow one road all the way to Kolkata," he says. "It's marked as their National Highway 2 so it ought to be good and if we keep the speed up to a decent average I reckon we can do it in a couple of days."

But not for the first time we are about to find out that there is a world of difference between the theory and reality of travel, especially in India.

India, Day Two ...

Delhi is a mighty big city. Its tentacles stretch out forever and as we pick our way through the endless suburbs, National Highway 2 (NH2) is revealed as a narrow strip of roadway, barely wide enough for easy overtaking. It is hemmed in on either side by a flotsam of shanty town-dwellers tossed out to the edge of the pond of socio-economics.

One in every five people in India lives below the poverty line of $1 a day, I had been told, and many of them seem to be here beside the NH2 as we begin our progress soon after dawn through the flat and dusty State of Uttar Pradesh. From the comfort of my fireside back in Newport Pagnell, I had often wondered what the poverty line looked like; it was like staring into a new circle of hell.

For most of the time we are down to a walking pace and the Kid can't get over it.

"It's got to get better soon," he calls out in exasperation. But it never does.

Despite its lofty title, the NH2 is pock-marked and pot-holed, a thousand imperfections made worse by the monsoon rains. But it is the sheer throng of people which slows us the most.

The road is like a magnet that attracts all the particles of life – a crush of dwellings, trading houses, haphazard shelters and tented awnings, all alive with the buzz and sounds of countless people.

Many of them spill into the road to take their chance, like us, among the host of bicycles and tricycles, and ox-carts and hand-carts and wandering cattle and putt-putt taxis nipping in and out, and the cacophony of hooting cars, lorries and buses trying to barge their way through.

The din and the smell of humanity are all around.

As the sun goes down we find a place to pause for breath.

Which Way Next?

"Only 400 km in 14 hours – if this is as fast as it gets there's absolutely no chance we'll make it in two days," the Kid lamented, arguing that we should press on into the night.

"Yes, but don't forget those warnings we had about driving after dark," I replied, recalling an earlier conversation with a couple of taxi drivers while we waited patiently beside them at a railway crossing.

There would be a lot more trucks about at night, they said, and from the sound of it, they didn't take any prisoners.

"Oh don't let's worry about that – they probably didn't know what they were talking about," said the Kid with his usual bravado.

He tossed me the keys. "Are you chicken or what?"

"Cluck, cluck," I thought to myself, accepting them reluctantly.

Four hours later, as we pulled up at Allalabad (not far short of our original target for the night) I was physically shaking with fear. Those taxi drivers had been right all along. It was mayhem after sundown on Highway 2.

In their halting English, one had said there was a law forcing lorries to drive only at night; the other had said that most of them choose to do so because they can travel faster.

Whatever the truth, the fact – as we soon realised – was that NH2 changed its character after dark from an over-crowded obstacle course into a racetrack for HGVs. Mad Max meets Death Race 2000, with an element of Carmageddon thrown in for good measure.

It was also a fact that there were very few cars about after sundown, and no family hatchbacks at all.

Instead, the road was now populated exclusively by 30-ton trucks, mostly of a certain age, hurtling along in convoys of a dozen or more, all following a leader who rampaged down the centre line, headlights blazing, hell-bent on scattering those coming in the opposite direction out onto the verges or beyond.

Poor GG. She may have braved the mountains of Afghanistan and bumped and bounced her way along some of the worst roads in the world, but this match was loaded.

"I would rather be in bed than dead," I said as we retired from the fray. NH2 one, Daewoo Challengers, nil.

We had managed only 600 km in 18 hours of driving.

India, Day Three ...

The carnage from the night before lies everywhere come the morning – a grotesque collection of smashed or burned-out cabs, cargoes and carcasses which litter the road or lie upended in ditches and trees.

It is a pitiful sight. For the most part, emergency services don't turn out unless there is thought to be a VIP involved; the dead or injured are usually left to lie in the wreckage all night. The warning of the impending danger they represent to other motorists consists, if anything, of a ring of stones laid in the road around the obstruction.

And now there is something else.

At the start of today, the Kid and I find a puzzle along our way. We have passed into Bihar State, still bumping and jolting on NH2, when we first see a patch of newly-laid asphalt running parallel to our road.

It never joins up with ours – just sits there alongside it, idle and empty – but at least it lifts Karaoke's spirits. "Might be some dual carriageway ahead," he enthuses. "Perhaps this road will improve after all."

Soon there is another stretch. And another. But the seductive frustration is the same because none of the passages connects with our roadway ... or with each other. They just seem to have been left there bereft and marooned.

"Hey," I say to the Kid, trying to lighten the tone, "this reminds me of one of those children's picture books where the roadworks are dots which you need to join up to complete the picture!"

What makes it more whimsical still are the large hoardings erected above each of the sections with a message in huge letters which says that the Prime Minister, Atal Vajpayee, views the improvements as his "dream project."

"Mmmm. In that case I bet he's not getting much sleep," quipped the Kid.

(We later learn that these roadworks are part of a five-year plan financed by the World Bank to improve NH2 and other major Indian roads. Each section of dualling is overseen by different nations – the Russians and Chinese amongst them – but the project is badly disjointed thanks to a chronic lack of co-ordination and planning. Paradise remains tantalisingly postponed.)

Which Way Next?

By the end of the day we have fallen even further behind schedule.

"Well, what do you think – fancy another game of night-time dodgems?" I queried the Kid, and this time passed the keys to him.

"Nothing more than a couple of hours then," he said. "My nerves just can't stand it."

We completed another 550 km today after driving for 14 hours.

India, Day Four ...

Things are looking up. Late yesterday, as we passed through Bihar State and into the hills of Jharkhand, the scenery had been getting greener and the road less populated.

Now there were paddy fields and farms and palm trees as the land rose higher and the air grew cleaner. We had even found a scenic spot to spend the night at a complex of tourist bungalows strung along the lake at Barhi.

With our oh-so-slow progress since Delhi we had fallen a further day behind schedule but we were still alive and that was all that mattered. Or was it?

"Late again? Oh well, what the heck," said the Kid nonchalantly as we warmed up GG for the day, but we are both so competitive I knew that, like me, he was only trying to hide his disappointment that our original schedule was falling further out of reach.

At first the going went from good to better. Crossing into West Bengal, we finally found our first piece of dual-carriageway – a glorious stretch for 60 miles (the one and only piece in this whole Indian trek as it turned out) where we could overtake with complete delight on the velvet-textured asphalt.

Then, all too soon, we were back to the ruts and potholes of the previous two days.

"Big hits", I called them, when whoever was driving failed to spot one of these craters in time to take avoiding action and poor GG's shock absorbers took another hammering.

I had taken to counting them. More than 12 a day and I reckoned I had failed to protect her. Today I was into double figures by lunchtime.

And yet. And yet. As we began the long approach to Kolkata, India's most-populated city, there was some compensation for our battered blue Goddess. Here, now, as the throng grew deeper on the swarming roadside, she would draw a crowd within seconds whenever we pulled up for our hourly breaks.

"I actually think she likes all the attention," said the Kid, cooing at her like she was another real person, after a spectacularly large group of inquisitive youngsters had flocked around her at a place I still can't name. "Anyone would think you were a film star ..."

His voice tailed off.

"There, you see, you've started talking to her too," I said.

By late afternoon we had arrived in Kolkata, across one of the big city bridges where the place used to end before the shanty town-dwellers hi-jacked the landscape, and we began again to ease our car slowly through the narrowing gaps between people and every imaginable form of transportation.

We stopped at a garage for a last fill of fuel.

"How much you want?" said the man in a uniform heading our way.

"Well, about 30 litres," I answered.

"Not fuel. Money," he said.

And then I realised. The man was a private security guard armed with a rifle. A thousand rupees (about £15) was a fortune round here. He took me over to the cashier who sat behind a plate glass window with a hole in it like they do at the bank.

"I make sure you pay money – then you get fuel," he said.

Welcome to Kolkata.

It took nine more hours to cover the 412 km on this fourth day of our trans-India trek, making a total of 41 hours for the total distance of 1560 km from Delhi to Kolkata on the NH2. The average speed worked out at 37kph, or something around three minutes for every mile.

Which Way Next?

India, Day Five ...

The last leg, a shortish, bumpy drive to the Bangladesh border from Kolkata, was remarkable only for the distance with which this historic city, once a powerful centre of administration for the British Raj and now the home of untold millions, stretched seamlessly on.

Distance driven so far: 15,000 km

Chapter 17
CINDERELLA GETS TO THE BALL

WEEKS 10 & 11: Siddhartha Kaul is Mr Asia for SOS Children's Villages. It's a very tough job. If we except Africa, most of the world's impoverished nations are inside his patch; in them subsist millions of destitute and abandoned children.

Helmut Kutin, the former protégé of SOS founder Hermann Gmeiner, a man who rose through the ranks to become its current president, cut his teeth in the region during the 1970s. He pioneered the development of the organisation across Asia, opening up scores of new villages and bringing help to thousands of youngsters in need.

For SOS it is a most important place; for Siddhartha Kaul, a larger-than-life character with a thick-set figure and heavy-jowled face, it is a huge responsibility.

Nominally he is based at the organisation's Asian headquarters in Delhi, capital of the world's second most populous nation (after China) and a busy enough place in itself for those who care for orphaned children. But most of his time is spent travelling – visiting and encouraging the key people who help to run the "business". He knows the best roads to travel, the places to go and how things work – often in strange and mysterious ways – from Karachi to Kuala Lumpur.

Fortunately for us, he is in his office on the day we come to call.

The Kid leads the questioning. Being in charge, amongst his many other tasks, of route-planning and map-reading, he is anxious to sift through Mr Kaul's knowledge and experience to find the best way for us to get from India to Korea and to complete this last leg of our Herculean task. He wants to know the best roads, the best border crossing points, entry visa and customs procedures, even the best boats where ferries might be needed – a kind of list of 'Dos and Donts' for those who Don't Know.

From time to time Mr Kaul stops to make some calls, consult his computer, and flick open his contacts book; at the end of an hour or two he has drawn us up a list which he is sure will lead us to our promised land.

Which Way Next?

"That's wonderful," we said as one. "We are so very glad to have met you."

We meant every word – and no doubt he did too. But what we didn't understand was that things have a habit of changing mighty quickly in Asia; and what is true today may just as easily be turned on its head tomorrow.

The first problem with our newly constructed plan materialised the very next day.

We had gone to the Myanmar embassy in Delhi to pick up our entry visas. It seemed a formality. After satisfying the regulations for 20 countries already, we thought we knew what to do: fill in the forms, carefully avoiding anything controversial like ticking the box to say we were political activists, or drug-smugglers with previous convictions, or even that we had recently glimpsed a thousand people who looked like Osama bin Laden; pay the money, leave the passports and then return to collect them a day or two later complete with a nice new stamp on the next available page.

But this time it was different. The man behind the thick glass screen was apologetic although he couldn't say why. He just pushed the passports with our money inside back under the grille and said: "You no visas. We reject. Very sorry."

Satish Kumar, Mr Kaul's dapper and quietly spoken chief assistant, who had been dispatched with us to lead the way, took up our case.

"We want to see somebody in charge," he demanded. "These Englishmen are on a charity mission to raise money for destitute children. They need to travel across your country, there must be some mistake."

But it was no use. "Rangoon refuse visa. Give no reason. That's all," said the man behind the glass. And, try as we might, we could do nothing to persuade him otherwise.

We were leaving the next day along Mr Kaul's suggested route across India, and then through Bangladesh to the border crossing with Myanmar at Cox's Bazaar.

"Oh well," I said to Karaoke as we assessed this new setback later in the evening. "Maybe they just got our papers mixed up with someone else's. Let's press on anyway and apply again at the border if we have to."

But we never did.

The news first came to our notice at a bookstore in Kolkata. "Bush orders trade sanctions on Myanmar," said a headline in that morning's paper and, reading down, we learned how the US President, in protest at the military junta's record on human rights, was to impose a ban on Americans buying goods that would deny their economy $1 million a day. To a western country that's a fleabite. Out here, it's crippling.

"Ah," I said to the Kid as we finished reading the story, "like everyone else at the moment, they're counting British and Americans as one and the same. So now we know. They haven't made a mistake over our visas and Mr Kaul couldn't have guessed; we've been caught up in global politics again."

We had another huddle. With China closed to us in the north and only empty ocean to the south, there was no way around Myanmar to get to Thailand, our next, and now very distant-looking, destination.

"Let's just get to the border," I argued. "We haven't come through all this to roll over and give in. If it's going to end at the gates of Myanmar then I want them to say it to my face!"

It was time to alert our charity partners and sponsors to the latest crisis.

"The problem is this," I wrote in an urgent email from the SOS Children's Village at Dhaka in Bangladesh, where we had paused to show off GG to the children. "Myanmar won't let us in, so unless anyone else can come up with a bright idea we'll just have to put the Goddess on a cargo boat from here to Korea (it will take about a month to get there) and call off what's left of our journey."

It was also time to put our team back in the UK on a crisis alert.

The temperamental periscope couldn't be trusted, so the email was sent into action again. "Fate of the trip now in balance," I said in a message explaining the situation to the base commander.

"Oh dear," came back his sorrowful reply. "Message understood… seven words I thought I would never hear."

The Kid's spirits were down, and so were mine. "All this way just to find ourselves thwarted on the very last lap. I can't believe it," I said.

But there was yet another twist to come.

Which Way Next?

It took a further week to find an answer – a week of frustration, of frantic negotiations with the Bangladesh customs regulators, with the help of Mr Kaul and Satish Kumar from SOS, a chunk of extra cash from our sponsors, the extraordinary determination of an international freighting company, a pilot named Igor from Uzbekistan and a Russian-made plane called Cinderella … but finally we found that there was another way to get over the problem of Myanmar and into Thailand after all.

Although we didn't know it, the idea of another airlift to help us back on track had been set in motion by Siddhartha Kaul even as were bumping and jolting across India.

Like Satish, his assistant, he had been stunned by our rebuff at the Myanmar embassy in Delhi.

Before we set off, our letter of understanding with SOS Children's Villages had stressed that they would not want to involve themselves with any issues that might arise relating to visas or other regulations. They would not have the time – or the staff – to help us with any such problems.

But this time they made an exception.

By the time we reached Dhaka, we found that the office there had already been hard at work for several days trying to find a solution, at Mr Kaul's instruction.

Shafi Mahmood, the bright young accountant, looking rather pleased with himself, pushed a bulky file across his desk at me on the first morning.

"I think I've found you something," he said.

"Cars like yours are a difficult cargo. No-one really wants to touch them. The size is awkward and they class it as dangerous because it's got fuel and a battery and well …" he lifts up his hands mimicking an explosion to emphasise what could happen if things went wrong.

"Then you have to think that you are not a regular shipper, you don't have any papers, you don't know the rules …"

"But Shafi," I said, cutting him short, "I thought you said you had some good news?"

"Yes well, I'm coming to that," he continued.

"It's still a long shot but this is Bangladesh, remember. Our country is poor and in this part of the world you can sometimes get things done

– for a price – that you might not be able to arrange somewhere else. Do you know what I mean?"

"Yes. Yes," I said, impatient to hurry him along.

"It would all be legitimate, you understand. It would be billed by a big-name company and they would take responsibility for the job, but I think I have found an outfit who know some people who could do this kind of job. The price will be high, and my guess is that you will have some serious problems in persuading our customs people to let you take the car out this way, but at least it's a possibility."

Cue yet another amazing escapade.

Abu Sayeed Khan receives us in his office in the centre of Dhaka. He is a chatty, likeable man with a ready smile who wastes no time in telling the Kid and me that he knows just about all there is to know about the freight forwarding business in Bangladesh. Mostly he handles shipments of clothing for America and Europe, he says – huge quantities of T-shirts and polo tops all boxed up and neatly labelled for the fashion market in the West and turned out for a cost of next to nothing in squalid apartment-block "factories" the length and breadth of this hot and overpopulated city.

"It used to be jute," he says with a certain sadness. "Not so long ago we were one of the world's biggest producers, but now the large companies have found they can make far more money from fashionwear."

We get around to talking about the car. "None of our regular shippers will touch it although, yes, I do know some people who might – but my biggest worry is our customs people here in Bangladesh. Have you any idea what you are up against?"

I said we hadn't the faintest idea.

"Well for one thing you will need special permission to get your car out on a one-off consignment like this and for another I have to warn you that the amount of officials and bureaucracy here will drive you crazy. Then there's the cost – you will have to make sure that certain … er … expenses are paid," he rubs the index finger of his right hand against his thumb in the unmistakable message that means cash will change hands.

"A little corruption eh?" I say with a wry smile.

"Well, let's just say that most of the people I deal with are used to receiving an express fee in cash to speed the process along."

"And how long is the process?" I ask.

"Hmmm. It could take a month, or a couple of weeks if you're lucky. But if you are prepared to come with me, follow what I ask you to do, and promise to keep a smile on your face, then we can probably do it in a day. It will be a long day, and I will be calling in every favour I'm owed, but yes, I reckon I can get you all the permissions you need in just one day."

I looked at the Kid and the answer was obvious from his face. We both knew too that this was our only chance.

"When do we start?" I said.

His face broke into a grin. "Tomorrow."

"And what about your flight crew?"

"Oh don't you worry about them - I'll get a call into that bunch right away. They'll be ready," he said.

True to his word, Sayeed met us at the offices of the Customs department next day. It was still early but already the place was busy with the tinkling tunes of mobile phones and the chatter of couriers, mostly young men with their arms full of papers and documents, scurrying about making appointments to see the variety of officials.

Once before – at the port of Aqtau in Kazakhstan after arriving by ferry across the Caspian Sea – we had found it took a full nine hours to get our car's paperwork through the scrutiny of Customs officers, the police and the military. But this was surely different. Here in Dhaka, without a military or police involvement it only needed the Customs authorities to approve our small request to put GG on a cargo plane and whisk her out of their country.

Our new friend Sayeed soon put us straight.

"The problem here is too many bosses," he said. "They are all paid by the government and they all want to protect their jobs. So when an unusual shipment like this comes along my guess is that none of them will want to take the authority for approving it."

"But what on earth are they afraid of?" I asked. "After all, it's not as if we're trying to smuggle something out of the country illegally, or trying to avoid paying duty on something we've bought."

"I know, I know …" said Sayeed, "there's no logic to it. But I know the way things happen around here and the trick to make this work is to get them all to sign. That way each one of them can feel safe in knowing that they have shared the responsibility and not taken it alone."

He gestured to the two of us. "Just accept it. Come with me and lay your story on as thick as you can if they ask you any questions." He gathered up the papers. Sayeed and his assistants had already prepared several impressive-looking batches of documents copied from anything that looked the slightest bit official.

After queuing at the first door for 30 minutes we were ushered into a dusty office where an elderly man sat behind a desk piled high with bundles of papers just like ours. He hardly looked up and continued meticulously copying the details from each piece of paper onto the pages of a large, dog-eared ledger.

Sayeed spoke first for all of us. "Sir, we have come to ask for your permission to let these people take their car out of our country. It's a very special case. They are raising money for charity – for destitute young children – and I ask that you give this your exceptional authority to help them carry on with their journey."

At last the old man looked up. There were some questions to the Kid and me and I thought we laid it on as thickly as we could.

There was a hiatus. His pen stopped writing for a minute and I guessed he was making up his mind.

"No," he said abruptly. "I don't believe the decision should be mine."

"Please," he turned his head towards Sayeed, "please go along to the second floor and ask them if they will do it there. I'm sure the answer should come from them and not from me."

We made our way outside. It had not been a very good start.

"Oh, don't worry," said Sayeed, trying to reassure us. "I told you it would be a long day."

It didn't get much better at the next office either. Or the next. Sayeed's prophecy was coming true.

We sat down to talk tactics. "I know what we'll do," he said suddenly like a hand of genius had just tapped him on the shoulder. "Let's change direction – let's ask them what they would be happy to sign."

Which Way Next?

We got the answer inside the very next office. "Write it out as a personal letter," said another featureless man who was busy copying information into a book, which looked remarkably like the previous one. "Address it to someone really high up and make sure it sounds like it has come from just the two of you."

Then "Oh," he added for good measure, "and why don't you say you have been through 21 countries already – with no problems at Customs in any of them?"

It was just the stroke of ingenuity we needed. The Kid and I wrote our letter out there and then to the deputy commissioner, clipped it to the top of another batch of papers, spent the next hour outside his office on the top floor, and watched in wonder as he unhesitatingly initialled his approval.

"British I see," he said in flawless English. "I went to school in London, you know."

After that, Sayeed's prediction turned out to be right again. There was a lot more waiting as we worked our way round the senior officers in the Customs department, but by the end of the day we had no fewer than seven signatures on our single sheet of letter paper clipped to the top of our pack and we had what we thought would be enough permissions to get our patient little GG out of here.

"All for one and one for all - you were absolutely right," I said.

"Come on, let's go back to my office and tell them the good news," said Sayeed.

But it was not to be. Well, not yet at least, for a fax was waiting on his desk when we arrived.

"Sorry - technical problems," said the short message. "Tomorrow's plane delayed five days."

"Ah, looks like we spoke too soon," I said.

Back at the SOS Children's Village, where we had been invited to stay while we sorted out our exit plan, there was only a resigned shrug of the shoulders from the Director, Theo Gomes. He had seen it all before.

As usual, GG had been an instant hit with the children and the Kid and I had already made plans with them to hold a first birthday party

Daewoo Challenge Photo Album

Part 2

Youngsters from the SOS Children's Village Kolkata dressed for the Banhan Festival.

Germany: A happy trio from the SOS
Children's Village Diessen.

Imst: High in the Austrian Alps.

Diessen: Children welcomed the Challengers on their first SOS visit of the trip.

FACING THE FUTURE WITH CONFIDENCE

These children now have hope and security thanks to the care of the 'family' of the SOS Children's Villages organisation.

Thailand: SOS Children's Village Bangpoo put on a great reception, welcoming us with flowers and a sing song.

Thailand's director Phahol Trangkineenad presented Richard (aka Elton John!) with this hand-painted scroll.

Vienna: A donation is presented by GM Daewoo, Austria.

© pic: GM Daewoo

Staff at the SOS HQ in Innsbruck turned out to cheer the Challengers but secretary-general Richard Pichler had to give the car a push.

© pic: SOS Kinderdorf

You're only here! Still a long way from Seoul.

This young boy at SOS Children's Village Tashkent receives our visiting card!

SOS Children's Village Hanoi: This, our 24th country and 11th SOS visit, was one to remember forever.

Baku: Village director Ugur Zeynally with some of the children in his charge.

Thailand: 'Welcome' say the staff and children at Bangpoo's wonderful village.

DANGER! MEN AT WORK

The author gets wired up for his writing duties on a park bench in Strasbourg, while Phil is in charge of route-planning and computer equipment.

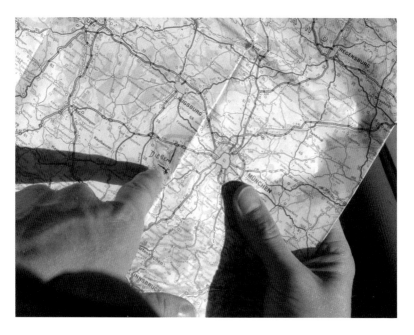

for her if our departure was delayed. So no problems there.

And Mr Gomes, a kindly man who had spent much of his lifetime running the Village and then expanding the number of SOS operations throughout his country, had only admiration for our day of effort at the Customs office.

"I'm just amazed that you achieved so much. I had been telling the others that it would take you a month," he confessed, before predicting darkly: "But don't be surprised if there are many more problems to come."

Next evening, when we found a moment to sit and talk, I asked him to explain.

"I know it must be difficult for anyone from the West to come here and understand how we live our lives," he began. "There's poverty and corruption and a great deal of bureaucracy, as you've already discovered.

"But you know, even if they don't have much, most of our people try to be helpful to each other and the strength of family ties is far greater here than for you."

I looked at him quizzically. "But what about the amount of violence and crime? Every day the papers are full of stories about people being shot and beaten in your city, and now (after news that same day that two opposition politicians had been assassinated in the street) there are to be strikes and threats of widespread demonstrations. I'm sorry but I can't help feeling that the situation here is deteriorating pretty rapidly."

He shrugged his shoulders. "It's certainly true that our people are volatile, but that's just our way," he said.

"Next week will be different, and then again the week after that. For you from Europe with your orderly lives and regular routines I guess it must seem strange, but we are used to it here and we have learned to cope with it."

It is still early in the freighting area of the airport when the Kid and I turn up with GG at the rendezvous with Sayeed and his colleagues for our re-arranged departure flight.

Mr Gomes was right, there had been more problems – and another late message from the cargo plane company had delayed our plans for a further 24 hours – but here we are now clutching our batch of forms with the seven-signature letter on top and with the Goddess all packed up and ready to go to Thailand.

"Any news yet?" I asked the Bangladeshi for the third time.

The phone is by his ear and there's a walkie-talkie in his hand. For several minutes now he has been alternatively firing questions into one or other of them as he seeks out any information on the progress of our plane and its mercenary crew.

He shakes his head. "No, nothing yet."

The clock ticks round. There's a kind of uneasy atmosphere as, little by little, the excitement we brought with us begins to fade. GG is doing her usual trick – pulling in a curious crowd of passers-by who want to know where she has come from, who we are, what we are doing and where we are going. It's a familiar routine, but it never fails to help pass the time.

The Kid shoots a glance my way. "Already an hour overdue – I don't reckon they're coming," he says with his usual Liverpool directness.

Suddenly there's another crackle on the walkie-talkie and Sayeed lifts it to his ear. I am guessing that whoever it is must be a long way away. Like before, there's a burst of staccato conversation, which I don't understand, and then our chatty Bangladeshi just listens.

The grin on his face tells it all. "Yes," he says, "this time they are really on their way."

Zia International Airport at Dhaka is no Heathrow, Detroit or JFK. By most world standards it would barely rate above small. There's a recently modernised terminal, the freighting and warehouse area where we have already spent most of the morning, several large administrative blocks and a collection of other ancillary buildings and offices.

By the time we get GG through the perimeter gates, out past the hangers and onto the runway, the big cargo plane has already been greeted by the team of workers who will refuel her, check out the maintenance list, and load her up with an assortment of crates and containers which are now – like our car – being delivered to her side.

Earlier in the trip we could have passed through half a dozen countries in the time it had taken to organise this moment. But now, after virtually two weeks of waiting, of false starts and broken promises, of gnawing frustration and pandering to the whims of bland officials, here at last was the way to outwit that refusal by Myanmar to let us into their country and the method by which we could hop over them and continue our journey to Thailand.

And it was quite a sight.

The Kid had climbed out of the car and was standing with Sayeed on the tarmac, his mouth agape.

GG's transport to Bangkok was a Russian-built Antimov 12 of an unknown age, with a fuselage that once was white but had now turned a murky shade of grey with accumulated dirt, a company name on the side which showed she was owned by an outfit in Cambodia, and a sign just below the pilot's cockpit which said her name was Cinderella.

"Hezzo," said a deep voice from behind us. "My name Igor da pilot. Is vat da car ve haff been telling about?"

Incredibly, there were still problems with officialdom and twice more, even as the big Antimov transport stood on the runway, we were summoned to get further signatures of exit permission from the airport's general director and his head of security.

But at last we said goodbye to GG. She had been all but smothered inside the big belly of the plane under the stacks of cartons and boxes of clothes, which would eventually find their way into the glitzy fashion stores of America.

Igor, the pilot-for-hire, turned out to be a Russian-speaking exile from Uzbekistan who had gone to Cambodia because there was no work at home and he had heard that the money was good. The rest of his crew, all dressed in jeans and sweatshirts, were his friends.

Poor GG. There had been no simple ramp to drive her up and into his plane, so 20 Bangladeshis from the airport ground crew fretted and strained to get her inside using fork-lift trucks until, finally, a high-rise platform did the trick.

"No vorry. Ve take good care of her," said Igor.

We go back to the SOS Children's Village for one more night. Tomorrow we will follow GG across to Thailand in a passenger jet, but right now, after 80 days on the road – and off it – this will be the first time that the three of us have been separated.

"Are you missing her too?" I tease the Kid who is by now sharing my fully developed habit of talking about our car in the personal sense.

"Yep, bit like losing a wart off your nose," he says, in that irrepressibly humorous Liverpool way.

Mr Gomes is waiting for us in his office. We want to leave early tomorrow so this is a chance to say goodbye. But first he has a warning…

"How did you get on at the airport today?" he asks, opening up the conversation.

"Oh fine, yes fine," we say, recounting again the story of Cinderella and Igor, her Russian prince charming.

There is a pause. Then he clears his throat nervously and says: "You remember I warned you that there could be more problems ahead…" (he didn't wait for an answer) "… well I've just heard that there is big trouble brewing for tomorrow."

I remembered the connection now. Just 48 hours ago, after their leaders had been shot dead in the street, political colleagues of the assassinated opposition politicians had gone on TV to pledge a day of demonstrations in their memory.

"Ah – they've decided to call it for tomorrow?" I guessed.

"Yes, and that means that travelling anywhere around here for the pair of you will be out of the question. There will be thousands of Bangladeshi people on the streets and, like I've already said to you, they are such a volatile lot that anything could happen. Last time, when there was something similar, I saw a man close to me in the crowd throw a grenade which killed some people."

There was no way to argue. "But we simply have to get to the airport," I said.

"Yes, I know. And I've been thinking about that. So here's what I suggest we do …"

The airport was only 30 minutes from the village. Even allowing for a two-hour check-in time, on any other day there would have been no need to leave before 11. But with today's strikes and demonstrations this was never going to be a normal day.

It was just on 9 o'clock when the privately hired ambulance arrived.

"Put your bags under the beds in the back and lie down like you've been hurt," ordered Mr Gomes. "Then we are going to close the curtains and put a couple of people in the front with the driver to make it look official.

"And now you must promise me something – whatever happens you must not get up and look out. You have got white skins and Western dress. It would not be wise to let anyone see some foreigners inside."

The Kid and I looked at each other.

"Great," he said, and we climbed aboard.

The early start was a brilliant idea. Mr Gomes, using all his knowledge of the city and its people, had planned it well. As yet, the main body of protestors were still making their way to where they had been urged to gather and make their feelings known.

The driver kept his siren wailing as we sped along. Three times we had to slow to a crawl as the swell of demonstrators spilled onto the road and, lying low inside, we could hear them chanting their slogans and waving their banners.

On the corner of one street, where the mood was starting to boil, several of them barged into the van and some muffled thumps rang along its side.

But we never had to stop. And, though sorely tempted, we never once looked out through the thickly-curtained windows.

"Hey," I said to the Kid as we roared in through the airport gates, "that's got to be one of the greatest escape tricks ever pulled. You couldn't write a better film script if you tried!"

"Yes," said the Kid. "you'd better pinch me please – or I'll think I've been dreaming."

Distance driven so far: 15,500 km

Chapter 18
BEK GOES MISSING

WEEKS 13 & 14: Thailand, and especially Bangkok, is at once a comforting and welcoming place for anyone who has just arrived hot-footed from the utter bedlam of Bangladesh.

I had spent a month here three years ago on another travelling tour and today I find the people no different – smiling, gracious and with a softly-spoken view of life which is so very opposite to the increasingly hard-nosed ways of the West.

In all of Asia, Thailand is emerging as one of the more stable places to do business. Unlike its neighbours, acts of terrorism are rare and its politics are lively rather than life-threatening. The national stock market is up for a sixth consecutive year and, as investors' money flows in, I notice the city's skyline has mushroomed from before with a flush of shiny-windowed new office blocks and headquarter buildings – the calling cards of global enterprise.

Our sponsors, taking our most recent excursions, exertions and exhaustions into account, have booked us into a luxury hotel to soothe away the pain.

The full 80 days allowed in our original plan have come and gone, leaving us still some way short in time and distance. The extra mileage on our Asian route, combined with the delays in Afghanistan and Bangladesh, means we can no longer be sure of a finishing date and all thoughts of rushing through the final leg to Korea now that we have vaulted over the Myanmar hurdle are thwarted when the Thai customs authorities decide to hold GG captive.

The strange story of a family hatchback with Belgian plates which has arrived in their country courtesy of the Uzbeki aircrew of a Cambodian company in a Russian plane minus its drivers and, probably more importantly, lacking any papers evidencing prior import/export approval, is something they haven't experienced too often. They need time to consult the rule books. They probably need to re-write the rule books.

For once we have a chance to act like normal visitors, and sightsee. Our trips to the Royal Palace and assorted Buddhist temples, together with waterboat expeditions on the Chao Phraya river to visit the city's alternative population of bankside dwellers and floating markets, help to ease the frustration that has mounted as our travel plans have been forcibly changed.

It gives us time too, to plan how we will manoeuvre our way across Laos and Vietnam, the last two countries before we send GG on a boat to Korea and our journey's end.

The Kid and I are discussing world events over breakfast on the riverside terrace at our posh hotel in central Bangkok.

"I see Man U lost 2-1 to Southampton at the weekend," he says with all the satisfaction of a lifelong Liverpool supporter gloating over a Manchester United defeat. The brief, inverted enthusiasm on display is very much his trademark.

We watch as the penny ferry, which constantly plies to and fro' across the fast-flowing Chao Phraya disgorges another hundred or so work-going types at the nearby jetty.

"Poor sods," he says. He doesn't speak much, but he says a lot.

Eggs for breakfast and freshly minted English language newspapers have been off our menu for so long that we are still revelling in the sheer sybaritic pleasure, but this stand-off with Customs has already dragged on for more than a week and I sense that very soon our jungle freshness, our open-road street smartness, will be quickly blunted by five-star luxury.

"I had a long chat with Chartchai (GM's Mr Fixit for that part of Asia) on the periscope last night," I said, vainly trying to drag his attention away from the match report.

"And" he questioned, vaguely interested.

"More bad thoughts about Laos I'm afraid."

"Oh?"

"Chartchai thinks we would be crazy to try and drive it. To prove the point he's been asking his contacts what they think and 90 per cent apparently agree with him."

"Mmmm," says the kid, lifting his gaze from the paper, but only briefly, "let's hope we get the car back soon then."

In truth, the case against driving across Laos had been stacking up steadily for days.

Perhaps Siddhartha Kaul had been practising kidology when he assured us that Laos would bring little or no problems when we consulted him about our revised Plan 3 at his office in Delhi a few weeks earlier.

The combination of politics and officialdom which we had run into in Bangladesh, and now here in Bangkok, has also prompted an email in the last few hours from Richard Pichler, the SOS boss back in Innsbruck, warning that these kind of problems would only get worse east of Thailand.

"Sounds to me like we could be in for another barrowload of paperwork trouble if we go to Laos – and that's without even thinking about the physical danger we would be putting ourselves in," I said.

As usual when we are about to travel into places we haven't been before – and that means most of them – the Kid and I start asking around to pick as much information as we can from those who know. And Laos is no exception.

One official view came from the US State Department's website. I had checked it myself. The statement, only just issued, unequivocally advised Americans to avoid travelling to Laos in general, and certain parts of it in particular, until further notice. In the last month, anti-government groups had bombed installations and attacked all forms of transport, it warned.

And the anecdotal evidence was worse. Bangkok is a mecca for travelling people and it isn't hard to find opinions. We had heard several stories about the kidnapping of foreigners in remote areas of Laos, and there was the recently frightening tale of a pair of motorcycling Austrians. They had been killed in the crossfire between rival forces not far from the route we planned to take.

We consulted the map for the umpteenth time. By crossing Laos at one of its narrowest parts we would need only to drive 500km before reaching the relative safety of Vietnam. That Vietnam can be described as relatively safe only serves to underline the potential dangers we faced.

The word on the street was that much of the journey would be through semi-jungle and along very basic roads where the heavy rainfall at this time of year would be a definite hazard.

The Kid was having none of it.

"OK, the roads may be bad but if we keep our heads down and stop for nothing we can do it in less than two days," he said.

It was certainly tempting.

The days were ticking by, but for once we had a chance to assess all the options and argue them out.

Time was one factor. "We are already so far behind schedule that if we put GG on a boat from here and send her around the South China Seas, goodness knows when we'll ever finish," I said.

And fan-mail was another pressure! With top-class email and telephone facilities available at our hotel, we had started to realise for the first time how many thousands of people all over the world were now following our trip and our many adventures through website and newspaper reports.

"Oh hell, now we've got a fan club to keep happy too," quipped the Kid.

The sponsors had a dilemma of their own.

"We have a big reception all lined up for you with government ministers at our Vietnamese factory in Hanoi," confessed Ken Hong, GM's PR consultant in Asia who had now been assigned to our account. "And there's a plan to hold a ticker-tape welcome for you down the main street in Seoul."

But then he added, in best PR-speak: "Obviously we would be disappointed at another delay and the welcome you will get may be a little thin if the story has lost its pace – but the choice can only be yours; we could never ask you to put yourselves in any danger on our account."

"Ah," said the Kid, "isn't it typical that we run into all this stuff just when the finishing line is in sight."

And that's how it was until two things happened in quick succession as we notched up our tenth day of enforced rest and relaxation in comforting Bangkok.

The first was news, confirmed at last, that dear GG was to be released from the Thai customs warehouse after heavy-duty lobbying at the highest level by the well-connected local SOS leadership, after the personal intervention of the director-general of Thailand's Customs Authority, after the payment of nearly US$1,000 in agents' fees, storage and handling charges, and after the signing of a surety for US$80,000 to cover the period our little Greek goddess remained in their country.

The second was a young hotel worker called Bek who made up our minds for us that we should drive through Laos after all.

I met him first.

At most big hotels like ours, the reception desk is a busy place. Upwards of a thousand guests, mostly, but not always as our presence confirmed, of the rich and famous variety, are a demanding lot. They want to know what's going on round here, how to get there, and a great deal more besides.

At least six people are on duty round-the-clock at our place and they have followed every individual episode of our 10-day long soap opera, sharing our mounting frustration.

Today I notice a new face at the desk, but already he has picked up the news of GG's imminent release on the hotel grapevine.

"What will you do now?" he asks.

"Get on our way again as soon as possible. Our next stop is Laos but we still haven't decided whether we can drive it. We think we may have to put the car on a boat and sail it round the other side," I explained.

He looked at me for a moment or two, then a gleam came into his eyes.

"Oh there's no need to do that," he said, "of course you can drive through Laos – take me with you and I'll show you how!"

And that was how Bek fell into the rabbit-hole and joined us in our very own Wonderland.

It was just another amazing stroke of fortune. He shouldn't have been at our hotel at all that day. His usual work was based in a small office at Bangkok's international airport where his job was to meet hotel guests arriving from around the world, help to smooth their path through all the procedures and see them safely off to the hotel on the courtesy bus.

But today was different; today, for the very first time, he had been told to report for duty at the hotel's main reception desk in the city centre because they were short of staff.

"My mother was from Laos, I speak their language and I have been there more times than I can remember," he said.

It was more than I could have dared to hope for, and already a plan was forming in my mind.

"What time do you finish tonight?" I asked. "If you can spare us half an hour I would like you to meet two important friends of mine – a graduate student from England, and a girl from Belgium with a Greek name who you will immediately fall in love with. I guarantee it."

Two days later and we are on the road once more.

Bek (his Thai name is so long that we have no option but to shorten it) has taken time off work to come with us.

He has quickly proved his worth by advising us of a better route across the troubled country and by organising, through his friends in Laos, a set of those all-important Customs papers that will get little GG in and out again.

We have struck a bargain: doubling the money Bek would have earned for his hotel work, covering his expenses and accommodation, settling a sizeable demand in cash from his Lao friends, and promising a substantial bonus if he can get us across the country in one piece.

"No need to bother," I cockily told the agent who had been looking into our boat-to-Vietnam option. "We have found someone to be our guide through Laos."

He listened intently as I told him the story of meeting Bek and what we planned to do.

"To find someone who speaks English, Thai and Lao, who is willing to go there with you and who knows the place like the back of his hand, is simply a miracle sent from heaven," he said.

I emailed the news to our base commander back at the World Media centre: "Will have a go after all. Leaving 4.30am to drive, repeat drive, Laos. Keep all fingers crossed!"

Thailand's border with Laos at Chong Mek is an immediate reminder that we are passing from one of the more affluent economies in Asia to one of the poorest.

Which Way Next?

The wide, well surfaced roads of Thailand with their Westernised shops, hotels and garages instantly peter out into a narrow, muddy avenue where tented populations of hawkers, trinket and food-sellers somehow gouge a living from passing travellers.

Long lines of trucks, achingly loaded with the sawn-up trunks of hardwood trees, snake into the distance as they wait to cross from the Laos side. The relentless process of felling the trees, de-foresting large tracts of jungle and increasing the danger from flooding and landslips, is devastating their land, but that's a hard case to argue when timber is the nation's main source of income.

Bek is out of the car, dealing with questions from the border guards and fending off the crowd, which quickly surrounds us like human bees smelling the scent of foreign money.

"I reckon he's paid for himself already," I say to the Kid as we brace ourselves for what lies ahead.

We drive without stopping for the rest of the day along roads that are strangely thin with traffic after the bustle of Thailand. In our usual style, we take hourly shifts at the wheel while Bek keeps up a constant commentary about the place from an uncomfortable perch in the back amongst the luggage, spare wheels and the assortment of bric-a-brac and general detritus we have inevitably collected during these last three months.

We are now in our twenty-third country. Discounting the ferryboat trips from Greece to Turkey, and across the Caspian Sea, and the two emergency airlifts across Afghanistan and Myanmar, our trusty Greek Goddess has covered more than 16,500 km along roads from Europe's slickest motorways to India's most potholed highways – but this land of Laos is yet another new experience.

"Doesn't it ever stop raining?" I ask Bek in exasperation as the wipers fight to clear the view through the windscreen.

"Yes of course, but not often at this time of year," he says.

Water has become a predominating feature – torrents of it pour from the gloomy heavens for hour after hour in this season of rain, and cascades of it rage down through the culverts and ravines into the mighty Mekong river whose chicken-toed tributaries split into a vast delta stretching from Thailand to Laos and from Cambodia to Vietnam.

Along route 13, which runs up from Pakse to Savannakhet, the helpful Japanese, under a generous agreement to help this impoverished nation, have supervised the construction of bridges and drainage work to keep the road open in all conditions. But we don't see many vehicles, or people, about; just a continuous land of lush vegetation, swamps and rice fields with simple, wooden houses, built on stilts, dotted among the trees.

Thirty years ago, when the Americans were fighting their ill-fated war in neighbouring Vietnam, US forces operated secretly from here in large numbers, flying their bombing missions to the north from airfields cut into the forest and training their men in the ways of jungle warfare. The Vietnamese too, used it as a thoroughfare for moving their troops up and down along what came to be known as the Ho Chi Minh trail.

"It's a sad fact, but in those dark days hundreds of thousands of Lao people fled their country to escape the battle – or to join it – and many of them have never come back," explained Bek.

This is the area where he grew up, he tells us; the place where his father – now a sergeant in Thailand's police force – met his mother, and where she died in an accident. It is also the region, he says, where American B52 bombers that failed to find their targets in Vietnam would jettison their payloads of high explosives and chemical weaponry before coming in to land at their secret hideaways.

Bek's mood is changing. He still keeps busy about his work – watching the signs in a language we can't understand to make sure we keep to the right road and warning us of potential danger spots or the likelihood of flood and river damage up ahead – but I am getting the feeling that something more is on our young guide's mind.

Night is beginning to fall but for the last couple of hours he has been urging us to keep driving to a place called Sepon further to the east.

"If we can make it there tonight, the journey to the border in the morning will be easy," he assures us.

But I'm not convinced we should go on and I take the chance to talk quietly with the Kid when we stop at a roadhouse to buy some water.

"Look, ignoring official advice not to visit Laos is one thing, but driving after dark on roads we don't know to somewhere we've never heard of is surely asking for trouble," I blurt out. And for once he agrees.

Which Way Next?

"OK, when you think the time is right, you just tell him and I'll be sure to go along with you," he says.

We have reached the crossroads with route 9, the road which will lead us eastwards to the border with Vietnam tomorrow, when we pass a bed and breakfast place.

"Change of plan, Bek. I reckon that's enough driving for one day so we'll stop here for the night and make an early start in the morning."

"But, but ..." he begins to protest, until the Kid comes in on cue throwing his full support behind my suggestion.

Later, when Bek's gone to his room, I ask the Kid what he's made of it. "I can't exactly say, but there was something definitely not quite right with him over that last hour or two in the car," he agrees.

"Oh well," I said, "let's just keep our wits about us in the morning and I expect we'll find out soon enough."

"...if he's still here," added the Kid ominously.

I don't suppose we will ever know if Bek told us the truth at breakfast next day.

We had guessed all along that the most dangerous part of our journey through Laos would come over the last 80 km – that was where the map showed us our route would climb steadily into the thickly wooded hills on the slow approach to Vietnam; it was the place where people had told us that road conditions would be at their worst; and – although neither the Kid nor I would ever admit it – if anyone was actually planning to set about ambushing two Englishmen who had very nearly, but not quite, completed one of the strangest journeys ever undertaken, this would be their best place to have a go at it.

"You need to get back for work?" I exclaimed as Bek told us sheepishly that he wouldn't be coming with us any further. "But what about our deal? What about your bonus?"

"I know," he said. "I'm really sorry but I talked to the hotel on my mobile last night and they told me straight out that if I didn't get back there right away I would lose my job. I just can't afford to risk it, I have a girl back there and a young daughter and ...," his voice tailed off in embarrassment.

It was a lame excuse, hardly plausible, but it soon became obvious that there was no use arguing. We just couldn't shift him.

I looked at the Kid after we had dropped Bek where he said his coach would stop.

"Know what I found in the guide book while you were fast asleep last night?" I said. "It took me a while, but it was all right there – that place he wanted us to go to, Sepon remember, it was apparently flattened in the American War by some B52s who didn't want to land with their payloads still on board. The book said there was all kinds of stuff including some napalm and chemicals used for stripping out the tree-cover. 'Yellow rain', the locals called it; it poisoned the water and killed their crops and...."

"OK," said the Kid, "I've heard enough. Maybe that's why he wanted us to go there so badly, maybe that's where his mother died, maybe he had some kind of revenge on his mind. But we'll never know now, so what's the use in wondering?

"Bek has gone and there's no turning back, so I say we should just get on with it."

And that was the way our final un-guided stretch began through Laos, a country that the world had been warned was officially too dangerous to visit.

Outside the car the rain is still tumbling down, sometimes in sheets, sometimes in a drizzle. But it just keeps coming. It gets worse as we start to climb into the hills that will lead us to the still distant border with Vietnam and, inevitably, the road begins to deteriorate.

Soon, we come across sections where whole chunks of the top surface have been washed away. It's obvious that those helpful Japanese haven't reached these parts yet and whereas yesterday their sturdy bridges had given us confidence over water-filled ravines, now there are only rickety structures barely the width of a single lorry to make our way across. The theme tune from Indiana Jones and the Temple of Doom plays eerily in my head on an endless loop.

And the traffic – not that there had been much anyway – is now reduced to an occasional truck that comes rumbling slowly towards us through the gloom.

"Oh GG," I find myself muttering, "if you want to have a break down, nervous or not, please don't do it now."

My head is all of a jumble. I am thinking again about the State department's warning; of Bek's abrupt departure, of 'yellow rain' and foreigners being kidnapped; of men in trees shooting at each other across the road and us being caught in the middle; of the engineer at last night's stop who said it would take forever to repair the roads around here because of unexploded mines left from the American war; and I am thinking about us – slip-sliding our way along a treacherous road in the middle of nowhere in a family hatchback that looks about as inconspicuous as an elephant in pink pyjamas.

I glance across at the Kid. When you've been travelling with someone for this length of time through some of the world's most inhospitable places there is a sensation in your stomach that oozes up in times of danger. I am feeling it now, and I know without asking that he is feeling it too.

Here's something else that I've discovered about the Kid – he thrives on fear. I knew it first when he got us through the mountains of Afghanistan with the most sustained piece of driving in conditions of unrelenting pressure that I had ever known – and he repeats the feat now in the hills of Laos.

His hands are tight on the wheel; no question now of changing places every hour; I know he will see this through for as long as it takes.

Within a few minutes we negotiate a bend only to find a fallen tree stretched across the road. It is just the kind of scene I have been dreading. There is no way round – just a detour off onto a muddy track into the trees and, hopefully, a later return to the road somewhere up ahead. If ever there was a place to set up an ambush, this is it.

I can see from the tracks that other vehicles must have made their way around the circuit sometime before because there are ruts of mud on either side and a pool of water of unknown depth lies in a muddy hollow at the bottom. But can we make it through? That's the question.

"Oh shit," I beat the Kid to the inevitable answer. "OK, I'll get out and go first and you just follow if I wave you through."

I am wearing jeans, a white sweatshirt and sandals. It is not the most sensible outfit for protection from the pouring rain, nor the best camouflage kit for a jungle setting where terrorists are known to roam, but somehow it doesn't seem to matter. I've reached a zone where the demands of the moment push all other considerations aside.

I squelch step by step along this muddy track, waving the kid and GG along when I think I've found a way that's safe and free from mines, trying to put all thoughts of unseen eyes and dangers from my mind, until we have reached the end of our detour. And then, with a final shove and slither, this remarkable little car of ours has found a grip from somewhere and clawed its way back onto the road.

I am wet, shaking, and more than a little frightened, but thankfully no-one has thought to shoot us dead. Yet.

A little later, while I am still scraping the mud and slime from off my feet, a man in a gold-coloured 4x4 draws alongside. The driver is from Laos and cannot understand our language but he sums up our situation in an instant – we are (a) English, (b) totally insane, and (c) we need his help.

He gestures us to follow him.

"It's that same old question – good samaritan or one of the bad guys?" I find myself asking the Kid again as we set off in the wagon's wheel-tracks.

"Well our luck hasn't let us down so far," he says.

An hour later, after this unknown hero has shepherded us through the maze of obstacles that was once a road, eased our path through mud-filled ruts and ushered us safely across flimsy bridges, we pull up smartly behind him at Lao Bao, the border crossing into Vietnam.

"Papers," says the Customs man, marching quickly towards us.

I think we know what is coming next.

"No, this is not in order," he says, walking slowly all round GG and inspecting her from front to back.

We can be totally certain he has never in his life seen anything like our gaily decorated car with its decals and stickers and hundreds of children's names scribbled across every inch, emerging from the mists of Laos.

"You will come inside and explain please."

Distance driven so far: 17,000 km

Chapter 19
PAPER CHASE

WEEKS 15 & 16: We fear the worst. The customs officer has little English, but all too soon he makes us understand that we do not have the right documents to get our car into his country and that obtaining them will be no simple task.

Vietnam is a staunchly communist country and while it is certainly true that in recent years there has been a slow opening of the door towards liberalism and enterprise, a centralised bureaucratic machine is still very much in place, and very much in charge.

"You need get papers Dong Ha," he says, pointing to a wall map showing Quan Tri province's principal town about 60 km away.

"But how do we get there?" moans the Kid, who has just parked our tired and muddy car out of the way under a nearby tree at the forcible direction of two armed soldiers with tall green-peaked caps.

"You get taxi. Car stay here," commands the official bluntly.

Our next, and ultimately historic, brush with international Customs law takes four days to sort out. In normal circumstances, it would have taken four weeks.

The officials at Dong Ha scour their rule books. A man from the department of foreign affairs is brought in to translate. After several hours they reach their verdict: only a signed approval from the Ministry of Security in Hanoi will do and they will send off the papers straight away.

"Send?" I query in exasperation.

"Yes," says the man from foreign affairs, "they will put them in the post tomorrow morning."

I spell out the scenario. "You mean they post the papers to Hanoi, Hanoi sends them round until they find someone to sign, then they post them back here, and finally you send them onto the people at Lao Bao to release our car?"

"That's it exactly," says Mr Foreign Affairs looking rather pleased that I have understood his efforts to explain.

"But that will take weeks," I complain. "What about faxing it all?"

"Not possible," he says. "The office has no fax machine, and anyway, for documents as important as this an original signature must be seen."

For any ordinary traveller, wanting to drive their foreign-registered car into Vietnam, the procedure would have been impossibly slow. But for us there is one very big advantage – we are sponsored by the world's largest car company with an assembly plant in the capital Hanoi, a large number of workers there and a staff already familiar with the government's corridors of power.

It took them three more days. Vidamco (GM in Vietnam) put their import/export manager and a team of drivers on the job. Twice driving through the night, they yo-yo'd up and down the country, ferrying the papers back and forth along the 700 km of road between Hanoi and Dong Ha. Finally, we are able to make a triumphant return to the border post at Lao Bao and gain the release of our abandoned GG from under her tree. There are new temporary licence plates to put on. They start with the number 0001.

"You make history. First car with permission under new system," says the man on the gate.

"Not bloody surprising is it?" says the Kid, straight to the point as always.

Lao Bao is one of the most remote border posts in Vietnam. The duty-free shop is run by a pleasant girl who has an odd assortment of goods on offer ranging from washing powder to packets of cheese biscuits and some high-octane rice wine which she siphons from a container that looks suspiciously like a can of spare petrol. It is such an eclectic mix that we inevitably come to the conclusion that most of her stock must be items originally confiscated by the Customs officers and now offered for sale at a total profit.

"So that's how they operate free market economics round here," I joke to the Kid.

Also in her armoury of entrepreneurial ability, the girl serves hot, thin tea from a flask she brings from home and there is a calculator in her purse to help with the complications of a money-changing service she offers for swapping US dollars into the spectacularly large-denomination national currency.

IIer strange emporium is our first taste of this new spirit of business enterprise now being encouraged in Vietnam, a country that will forever be remembered as the battleground of an attritional war in which more than a million Vietnamese and 50,000 Americans died, and the lives of countless others were ruined.

But in this land of many surprises, we soon find another – the roads are absolutely lethal.

From our entry point roughly halfway up the country we travel north along the 1A road, a principal highway linking the industrial centre of Ho Chi Minh City (Saigon) in the south to the controlling and administrative capital of Hanoi. It is a two-lane highway populated by hay-making farmers, wandering cattle, stray dogs, thousands of cyclists without lights, a succession of ancient vehicles labouring their way between fields, and a host of pedestrians apparently determined on an early demise.

For the Kid and me, who have survived the near-miss games of driving in Paris, the race-track of Rome, the suicide Olympics of Athens, and a good deal more besides, this is an Oriental revelation.

"It's right up there with the most dangerous," says the Kid as he hits the brakes with a squeal to avoid an unlit bike with a young girl on board which suddenly appears in our headlights from a gateway.

And there is worse to come.

When we finally reach Hanoi, little GG is instantly engulfed in a tidal wave of scooters, mopeds and motorbikes with Japanese names like Suzuki, Honda, Yamaha and Kawasaki, which buzz around the busy streets. They are the universal transport in this frantic city, a cheap and nifty way of getting about for the entire population, young and old alike, travelling to work, going out, fetching the kids, buying the groceries …

I find myself keeping count in a "most-people-on-a-moped competition". The result is four, and the man at the very back has positioned himself to face the traffic coming up behind. The sight is completely disorientating.

But this is really what we came here for – a visit to the SOS Children's Village on the city's fringe which turns out to be one of the most memorable days in this long, long journey of ours.

GG has been looking forward to it. After her enforced detention under the tree at Lao Bao, and the dangers of our journey along road 1A, she is refreshed and ready for more.

Before we set out for the village I make a quick inspection. She is, in herself, a collection of everything we have been through together, and today I can't help thinking that she looks every bit the global traveller.

We have put nearly 18,000 km on her clock and although she has taken a terrible battering she is still virtually unbent, unbloodied and certainly unbowed.

There's a dent on one side at the back to remind us of Afghanistan, one glassless spotlight to recall the near-miss with a lorry in India, stickers with coded numbers that record the airplane flight from Bangladesh, souvenir symbols to remember the aircrew who flew her over the sandstorms to Kabul, scores of signatures and goodwill messages scrawled across every panel and now, the latest thing, our historic new "number plate" printed in big black type which has been fixed to her windows front and back.

"Shall I give her a quick wash down?" says a helpful young porter at the hotel before we set off, eying the dirt down her sides from yesterday, and Laos, and Thailand, and a lot more places than he could possibly dream of.

"No, that won't be necessary." I said. "I like her just the way she is."

We arrive at the village after a bit of stage management. We have come to realise that it has to be that way in any large city where there are bigwigs waiting for us at a certain time and we can't be late, so a guide has led us there early to skulk around the corner until we can make our grand entrance at precisely the right moment.

After more than a dozen visits to these villages the Kid and I are beginning to feel like old hands at them – but this turns out to be quite the best welcome we have had so far.

Around 100 children burst into applause as we come through the gates, ushering us to drive across their yard and under an enormous horseshoe-shaped structure covered in balloons, which is the centrepiece. There they crowd around to offer so many bouquets of flowers that little GG is in danger of being smothered beneath a multi-coloured blanket of blooms.

Which Way Next?

The TV cameras and their lights are here, so are the newspaper reporters of Vietnam's press, free for once to write a happy story without the supervision of government officials. So are the executives of Vidamco with their sombre suits and silky ties, ready to present a generous donation to Village director Do Tien Dung, a kindly man with a boyish face. And so too are some of the most artistic children in his care who will perform traditional dances in their finest clothes and entertain us all with a lively puppet show.

The village "mothers" line up to shake our hands. They had begun taking in orphans and destitute children to this wonderful place after the American War, to give them life and hope and a future. They too have little English, but words are not needed for what they want to say to us, and us to them.

Later, after a motorcade through streets thronged by the motorbike hordes, being filmed for tonight's television, and a tour of the sponsor's factory in the heart of town, we are taken to a restaurant to celebrate the day.

Someone brings in a borrowed TV.

"Hey," says the Kid, feigning embarrassment after we sit through seven minutes of today's events on the prime-time evening news, "we've never had that much coverage before."

Our host, Jung In Kim, Vidamco's general director, smiles across the table.

"This country has gone through so much trauma, so much pain. A story like this is a happy story, it's happy for everyone, and that's just what we need."

"Everyone wanted to make it a special day."

"And you all did," I replied. "You certainly did."

I have put a call in to our sponsors on the periscope. They are rather pleased with us, it seems. All that talk in Thailand about putting GG on a boat to avoid the drive through Laos apparently upset them and now we learn the reason why: there's a deadline for us to get to Korea because they want to display her talents at a big motor show there. Now that we have caught up some days – despite our problems at the border – we are back on track to get her there in time.

It's not possible to drive all the way to South Korea (well, not from the direction of our final Plan 3) so we will need to put the car on a boat at Haiphong, the port near Hanoi, and our sponsors will take responsibility for transporting her on from there. "You are almost in our back yard now, so you can just sit back and let us take the strain," smiled Ken Hong's voice bouncing down from the satellite.

"Right you are then," said the Kid when I gave him the news, "why don't we take in some sight-seeing while she's sailing across the seas to Korea?"

He's been checking with the hotel's enthusiastic travel desk.

"If we fly there to meet her we can catch up with the boat in a day – and that will give us another week here to look round some more of Vietnam. What do you say?"

Vidamco are pleased with us, too. They got so much publicity out of our visit to the SOS Children's Village that they offer to finance our proposal for a bit of rest and relaxation.

The Kid is quickly back in his role of chief navigator and route-planner as he pulls his head up from the pile of maps, books and brochures spread around him on the floor.

"Let's do two things," he says. "We can float gently round the islands of Halong Bay for a couple of days, and then go up to the hill tribes of the north to put us back in jungle mood for the final lap."

There was no arguing with that.

It's no wonder that tourists have been avoiding Vietnam, considering its recent record of wars and battle. Three serious conflicts – the ending of a century of French colonial rule at the siege of Dien Bien Phu in 1954, the American War through the 1960s and early 1970s, and the repelling of an unwelcome invasion by the Chinese in 1979 - have all kept visitors away; plus the restrictions of a communist regime which frowned haughtily on the ways of the West.

But that's all changing now.

After a period of peace lasting more than 20 years and the collapse of communism with the break-up of the old Soviet Union, a gently-does-it transition towards more liberal views and private enterprise is under way. Russian is no longer the compulsory extra language at schools (English has mostly taken its place) and a lure for the hard currencies of foreign tourists is being carefully laid.

Halong Bay is one of the prize surprises that awaits the visitor.

We board the converted junk in Haiphong harbour round about lunchtime on a day of cloudless skies and sizzling sun. We've just said goodbye to the pretty Greek Goddess who's been a part of our lives virtually day and night for the last three months, and I have the distinct impression that the Kid and I are feeling rather sad.

"Seems funny her sailing off one way while we sail off in another. Bit like ships departing in the night," he says, almost making a joke.

But we needn't have worried.

Halong Bay is a hugely restful place for two world-weary travellers who set out a long time ago on a shopping expedition and haven't yet reached the checkout. It's a soothing place of calm waters and quiet coves where only the sound of a clinking beer glass disturbs the peace.

Two German girls, an Irish couple living in Hanoi, and a friend of theirs over from Dublin, are our companions on this, er, junk-et.

There are said to be 3,000 islands in Halong's relatively undiscovered bay just off the north-east coast of Vietnam – wonderful, mysterious, uninhabited clumps of wooded limestone which rise up sharply from the sea like rows of gappy alligator's teeth.

We don't see more than a tiny percentage of them. In fact, in the general scheme of things, I don't suppose we see many at all. But we spend 24 glorious hours idling gently through mill-pond, green-blue waters stopping at places that take our fancy for a swim, or getting off to stretch our legs and explore some caves, or sitting on deck with a beer glass in hand watching the evening sun sinking and reminiscing.

And maybe, I'm thinking, we're not missing GG so much after all.

A couple of days later and our expedition to meet the hill tribes of the north-west is an altogether different experience.

We journey up into the high country near the Chinese border by train, and then by Jeep, and finally on foot. This is a land that tourists are only just beginning to find; a land where the hill tribes – or minority people as the guide book describes them – have lived and worked their opium and rice crops for centuries.

At first we pass them on the rough and tumbling road which winds through the foothills of the towering Mt Fansipan, the highest peak in the whole of this part of Indo-China - people from the *Black H'mong* tribe, distinctively dressed in dark clothes and leggings with black, cylindrical hats, straggling along on their way to market with panniers of rice and vegetables.

The valley below is a wondrous sight with clearings sliced into its thickly-forested sides revealing an amazing precision of hand-dug flights of light green steps where these hill people cultivate their life-sustaining crops of wet and dry rice.

We meet more of them as we pass along the road to Sapa, a market town where the minorities go. Now they are *Dao* people from further north, a handsome tribe where the women adorn themselves with red and white topknots that look for all the world like Father Christmas hats.

Our planet overflows with the plight and disillusionment of oppressed minorities who have lost their land, their heritage and finally their dignity. But here at least – and for as long as it takes the inexorable tide of tourism to engulf them, I suppose – the people are still going about their daily lives, just like their parents and grand-parents before them.

We walk along the valley floor, through villages where children still scrabble in the dirt with their neighbours' chickens for a bowl of corn, where water from the mountain stream drives the family's threshing hammer, and where the houses are made from thatch and wood. It is truly an education.

Next day we travel to Bac Ha, a bigger town with a larger market, where the people of the *Flower H'mong*, holding fast to their lifestyles with tradition and pride, are parading in a peacock splash of multi-coloured dresses and headwear. They smile at total strangers like us. There is no bitterness or resentment or envy. And they smile a lot.

They have brought their hard-worked items for sale: hand-sewn bags, purses and hats, cotton material for clothing and garments, all kinds of fruit and freshly-picked vegetables, fish and shellfish, and a squealing livestock of pigs and goats, cattle and dogs.

We come back on the train with our hopes alive that here in this half-forgotten land of beauty, the hill people of Vietnam may survive the unforgiving waves of progress.

Which Way Next?

The Kid has been thinking about that.

"I'll give them another 10 years, maybe 15 at the outside," he says.

Next day we board our plane to catch up with GG in Korea. Journey's end is at last in sight.

Driving distance so far: 17,800 km

Chapter 20
GRAND FINALE

WEEKS 17 & 18: Our final frustration is every bit as agonising as the rest.

The boat taking our little Greek Goddess to Korea is delayed by the typhoon Maemi, one of the worst to hit the region for many years. It roars up the China Seas leaving a trail of mayhem across everything in its path. The journey by container vessel should have taken a week, but now we hear that she has had to run for cover into Hong Kong's sheltered harbour and ride out the storm for an extra three days.

We also put back our flight from Hanoi and arrive the day before the re-scheduled boat is due to dock at Pusan at the southern end of the Korean peninsula. But even that turns out to be too soon because the port has been ravaged by the violent seas and the wrecked facilities, including several of the unloading cranes, bring a further delay of two days while the backlog of shipping, which stretches out across the bay like a maritime traffic jam, waits idly in line for its turn to deliver.

Finally, late into the night of Thursday, October 2, the container ship *South Seas Aurora* with GG tucked safely on board ties up at Pusan's battered dockside. Now, at long, long last, we can say that the three of us have reached Korea!

It is 115 days since the journey began from faraway England – a great deal more than the 80 days which we had so boldly predicted.

But that was before Plan 3, our rescue by the Hercules in Afghanistan, Cinderella's airlift from Bangladesh to Thailand, the excruciating delays of Customs clearance procedures, and now the devastating effects of a typhoon. We had built in two weeks for contingencies and emergencies; in the event we needed six. It also means, worst of all, that we have missed the opening of the Pusan International Motor Show ...

This year's exhibition of cars at Pusan is everything that a visitor might expect from a place which projects itself as the "most dynamic city in the world" and from a nation which boasts five of the leading car manufacturers on the planet. Over the course of the next 10 days, up to a million enthusiasts are expected to pay homage to the glitzy new products of an increasingly motor-mad society in the futuristic Bexco arena, which looks about the size of Wembley Stadium (before Wembley Stadium fell victim to the bulldozer).

"I think it's over there," says the Kid, straining – even with his greater height – to spot the GM Daewoo stand above a large, excited and awestruck crowd which has gathered round the display of a rival firm that features several girl models who are wearing not very much and are draped around a selection of gleaming new cars in such a way that they make even the door handles look sexy.

We struggle, him and me, to get through the adoring masses.

"Yes, yes – that's it," he says excitedly as we get within range, "I can see…"

But he doesn't finish the sentence.

We, too, are staring now; straight at the giant, full colour screen that forms the backdrop of the Daewoo display. "Welcome to the Challengers," it says across the top in sky-high letters.

But we, the Challengers, are not yet here to receive the welcome.

If only the *South Seas Aurora* had docked just 24 hours earlier, the Kid and I and our remarkable little family hatchback would now be on the stand in person – a trio of muddy adventurers, just arrived as conquering heroes from a drive around half the world, flashbulbs popping, girls a' plenty and the star attractions.

But today it is a day too late.

We had hassled the authorities in Thailand, driven when we shouldn't have in Laos and made history in Vietnam, but seemingly it has all been for nothing. Typhoon Maemi has seen to that. Arriving in the middle of last night was one day too late for our special Greek Goddess because today was the opening of the big exhibition. The stands are up, the crowds have arrived and there is no way the organisers can just open the doors and let us drive in.

GM Daewoo, our sponsors, had issued instructions as soon as they knew that little GG wouldn't beat the deadline but it was too late to dismantle half the stand, with its premature notice of welcome. In fact, they would want us to keep out of the way for the next few days until they could organise something equally appropriate to mark our arrival, they said.

"Oh well, let's go down there in disguise and see what might have been," the Kid had said. And I agreed.

Which is how it came to be that the two of us are now standing, mouths wide open, in front of this super, welcome-home-heroes display – him wearing dark glasses and a T-shirt with the logo of a fairly low-profile insurance company on the front, and me in my Elton John lookalike party outfit with the over-sized, golden $ sign around my neck and a pair of red checked surfer shorts.

"Cor, won't you just look at that," says the Kid as we gawp up at the mural-style, multi-coloured map that charts all the places we've been, complete with inset photos and the flags of 25 nations. It stretches right the way across the Daewoo stand and it is, well, as big as a small house.

In front, directly below the legend, which says to welcome us, is a Kalos car. True, it is new and nice and shiny and its light blue metallic finish is impressive in the spotlights. But, let's be real, it is most definitely not a patch on our GG.

"It's a bloody impersonator. What a cheek!" says the Kid. And I feel the same about it too.

"Let's take some pictures," I suggest, trying to make the best of it. "Then we'll have some proof that we were actually here on the opening day. We've risked our lives to make it to the show on time, and even if a million people don't know that, at least we will!"

Thinking back, I suspect it was the Elton John wig that gave our game away.

We had just persuaded a quizzical onlooker to take a photo of the two of us – exactly where we might have stood in fact, greeting visitors and introducing them to our famous car until typhoon Maemi had her say – when a voice came from somewhere at the back of the crowd.

"Is there anything I can do to help?"

It came from a smiling, sharp-suited Korean man who was heading our way.

"I'm Hyun-Il Lee, director of marketing services and in charge of the display. Er, would it be this Kalos model that you are interested in?"

Which Way Next?

I looked across at the Kid who was trying his hardest not to burst a blood vessel laughing.

"Well yes, I suppose we are," I said, feigning interest.

And now we find out why Mr Sharp Suit is not the director for nothing. His eyes are going over my shoulder to the display of pictures behind. I can see him looking from one to another, and then another. I can almost hear his brain ticking.

"But aren't you ...?"

"That's torn it," I chuckle to Karaoke. "I think our cover's just been blown."

We have our grand finale six days later. Again, the days in between are a frustration for the Kid and me. The sponsors want to wait for the media to grow tired of talking about the motor show and to begin their hunt again for something fresh. So we keep our heads down at a place where I can busy myself with Internet research, usefully delving into background on the Daewoo name's colourful history in Korea, and hiding GG away from prying eyes in an underground car park.

Our story is a good one in the newsworthy sense; already it has had huge media and TV coverage in virtually every country we have visited. And now it will have a happy ending too.

The official finish of the marathon gets under way the following Wednesday, October 8.

We have been kept in the dark for the most part about what is planned, but when a big coach adorned with banners arrives at our hotel, literally to set the wheels of celebration in motion, we get the feeling that this will be quite a day.

GG comes up from the car park with her frog's-eye spotlights blinking in the bright autumn sun. The Kid and I can't resist talking to her now she is one of the family again.

"Hey, you look really good today," he says, patting her on the engine cover. "This is the big one GG, this is what we've come all this way for." And I swear I can see her bull-bars break into a grin.

It's about 30 minutes to the factory of GM Daewoo Auto and Technology at Bupyung on the overlapping city fringes of Incheon and

Seoul, and our eye-catching convoy turns heads all the way as we follow behind the big-bannered bus through streets that are becoming busy with the morning rush.

GG is in her element. Covered in the mud of many nations and decked out with her stripes and stickers, she is a wonderful oddity among the comfortable saloon cars in this country of economic miracles.

"Give them a wave," I say to the Kid as a group of office workers stop and stare while our strange procession passes by. "I don't suppose they can believe their eyes."

And that was just the start of it.

The Bupyong plant has been chosen as the final destination of our journey because it was here that GG rolled off the production line a little more than a year ago, and as the coach peels away from us outside the factory gates we soon find out just how much it means to the workforce to see her back.

"Hell's teeth," says the Kid with his usual short-and-pointedness. He has taken a peek at what's inside.

Over the entranceway another huge banner bids us welcome – this time for real and in person – while a marching band of 30 girls, smart as soldiers and twice as pretty in a cascade of white and blue uniforms, strikes up a tune to lead the way.

Inside, along the half-kilometre of entrance road, we begin to learn what it's like to be a celebrity. The morning shifts from two of the factory sites have stopped work to join the fun – nearly 3,000 of them – lining the street on either side waving and applauding as we drive slowly by. Now one group breaks into a cheer. Now another – and soon the whole crowd is letting us know how pleased they are that we've brought their GG safely home.

I have switched on all the lights to increase the dramatic effect. "Not a bad homecoming for a second-hand hatchback," I joked.

"Hell's teeth," says the Kid again, scarcely able to believe what his eyes and ears are telling him. "It's better than the finishing stretch of a marathon at the Olympics."

I call across to him: "Ah, but this one's for us – all three of us. Think of it a lap of honour if you like, and doesn't it feel just great to be a winner?"

Which Way Next?

We are nearing the top of the service road. I have been weaving the car along slowly from side to side so the two of us can shake the host of hands stretched out in congratulations and good wishes, but now I pull up behind the band as we reach the main reception area where a group led by Nick Reilly, the chief executive, and his senior managers is waiting.

And here is a flower garland to go around our necks, and a bottle of something fizzy to shake in the air, and a lectern and microphone to make our speeches.

Mr Reilly, the man who not so long ago was in charge of GM Vauxhall's plant at Luton – the "Hatter's" town north of London where we took to the road just over 17 weeks ago – is starting things off. I can hear him saying things like …"remarkable journey" … "such determination" … "amazing story" … "proud of you both" …

But I'm finding it hard to take it all in.

And now it's my turn. There's a lump in my throat where my oesophagus ought to be and I haven't prepared anything to say.

My mind is all of a jumble, but what can I do?

Say something nice, I'm thinking; something to thank them all; something to say how we've looked forward to this moment; something to say what a journey it's been; something …

I look across at GG to find some inspiration. She is there just where I had stopped her, right in front of everybody, every inch the main attraction, her doors still open, headlamps and spotlights full on, the hazard lights still clicking …

But now an awful thought is entering my head. "Oh whoops," I explain as the largest audience of my life draws in its breath. "I've just realised that I've left the lights on."

It's the kind of thing that means more to the workers in a car factory than anywhere else – and another loud cheer goes up as I walk across to turn them off. " Oh GG," I whisper, "this is definitely not the day to let your battery go flat!"

And now the tension is broken and my shoulders can relax. The right words come easily after that.

The rest of our celebration day is a blur. There's a press conference with TV crews and camera bulbs flashing, a great many people are wishing us a great many things, there's a pile of gifts, a lunch in the staff canteen and a tour of the factory where men and machines combine to create one of the most productive and efficient car construction operations in the world.

Later, there is a reception at the house of Charles Humfrey, the British Ambassador, and another where we can tell our story to a large group of motoring journalists and specialist writers. Hanspeter, the man in Zurich whose decision made all of this possible, has flown in to join the party.

But the highlight for me comes right at the end when the Kid and I slip out for a meal with Nick Reilly and Rob Leggat, one of his closest aides.

This is a rare opportunity to talk with the British-born chief executive of our sponsoring company and it gives me the chance to ask him about some startling information which had been unearthed for me by the Internet during our wait "under cover" for today's grand finale.

We find ourselves a table at the back of a half empty restaurant away from the glamour of Seoul's lively centre. At first the conversation is all about our trip. Like Rob, his boss is interested to hear our first-hand accounts of the journey and he questions us closely about the dangers we faced in Afghanistan, our escape from the rioters in Bangladesh, and the driving through Laos and across India.

He listens intently to every detail. At 53, Nick Reilly's approachable style and successful record with GM have rocketed him into the very top flight of management (and the highest position of any non-American) in the world's largest car-making company.

Already, in just his first year after taking the helm at GM Daewoo, he has increased their share of the highly-competitive car sales market in Korea by 7 per cent, stepped up production at their three major factories, and launched several new models to extend their range.

Little GG would also be pleased to hear that the Kalos will soon be exported to nearly 100 countries around the world and that new variations, including a three-door and a diesel-engine version, are to be launched in a couple of years time.

Which Way Next?

"It all sounds like a tremendous beginning," I said, "but didn't you wonder what on earth you were getting yourself into after the scandal surrounding Kim Woo Choong?"

"Oh, you know about that?" he queried.

So I told him what I had discovered in the files – how the news back in 1999 had been full of garish headlines about Mr Choong, the Daewoo boss who had simply disappeared one afternoon after setting off for a meeting in China, taking with him a large fortune in cash and leaving investigating accountants to later discover that his company owed $65 billion it couldn't pay.

"Well yes," said Nick, "it certainly left a big mess to sort out, and for the year before GM stepped in it was a very damaging time with so much uncertainty. Not surprisingly, sales went down dramatically, some of the dealers jumped ship, and the fabric of the company was badly disrupted."

But what about the scandal of Mr Choong?, I wanted to know. (He is still in hiding with a number of accusations against him alleging fraud and embezzlement.) "Hasn't what happened caused a big problem for the Daewoo brand's reputation?"

"I can't be sure about the rest of the world, but here in Korea they take a pretty phlegmatic view about it," he said. "Some people undoubtedly think he may be a villain – but a great many others still see him as a hero who built up a huge company from next to nothing, creating thousands of jobs and a great deal of wealth for their country."

The conversation went quiet for a while and it gave me a chance to stack up the background in my head.

"So you are trying to resurrect a company that went bankrupt, rebuild sales from a stagnant year, piece together a global network that split itself into pieces, and repolish a brand name tainted by the scandal of a founding figure who is still apparently wandering around the world with a big chunk of the company's cash?"

"Er, well yes," said Nick, "I suppose you could put it like that."

"Then it isn't us that's had to face the Challenge of a lifetime," I joked. "It's you!"

Total distance driven: 18,350 km

And finally ...

On Sunday, October 10, Richard Meredith and Phil McNerney took their Kalos car to the SOS Children's Village at Daegu in South Korea, which was that day celebrating its 40th anniversary.

Daegu was SOS's first children's village outside Europe and therefore became an important milestone in the development of Hermann Gmeiner's dream of building a worldwide organisation.

A cheque from the Challenge sponsors – swelled to 60,000 euros by an extra contribution from GM Daewoo's parent company in the USA – was presented to SOS Children's Villages by Chong-Su Kim, managing director (corporate affairs).

SOS Children's Villages in Daegu, on behalf of the Korean national association, then immediately handed it to their colleagues in Nepal, one of the world's most impoverished nations, saying: "Your need is greater than ours."

The money will now help towards the building costs of a new SOS Children's Village at Bharatpur in Nepal's Chitawan valley.

Richard Pichler, secretary-general of SOS Children's Villages, said in a personal message to the British adventurers: "This generous donation will make a tremendous difference to the lives of children in Nepal. We are delighted about this great achievement. On behalf of the worldwide SOS Children's Villages organisation and especially the children – thank you!"

On November 9, Richard Meredith and Angela Sherman officially opened Daewoo House at Bharatpur on behalf of the Challenge team during an inauguration ceremony for the new village attended by guests from many parts of Europe and Asia.

Which Way Next?

APPENDIX 1

The following articles are from a selection specially supplied to leading journalists around the world who followed and reported on the progress of the Daewoo Challenge story

Laid-back Russian girls pep their finances

You see them coming down from Russia at the border crossings – plush Mercedes, big BMWs and sleek new limos in the executive range.

Behind the smoke-tinted windows sit a couple of large gentlemen with square shoulders and close-cropped hair. In the back are two or three fit-looking girls who are definitely not dressed for a day at the office.

The oldest trade in the world is alive and flourishing and has a new lease of life courtesy of one of the lesser-known trends of the post-Soviet economy.

We are waiting patiently like the rest of a queue of more conventional travellers at the border crossing from Georgia into Turkey while officials make it their business to stretch the approval time for paperwork to ever-increasing lengths.

But when the big BMW rolls in with its smoked-glass anonymity and tall radio-phone aerials there is a noticeable quickening of the pace.

Time is money to these kind of passengers and like the VIP lounges at international airports there is a fast-track system to get them through the red tape rigmarole. Or, at least, there appears to be. What seems obvious, too, is that this kind of shipment arrives on a regular basis.

A decade after the break-up of the old Soviet Union, newly-independent countries like Georgia and Azerbaijan are finding themselves as go-betweens on the lucrative run of call-girls down from southern Russia to the resorts and business centres of the Black and Caspian seas.

Ironically, for some countries which were so recently ruled by Soviet masters, there is a surprised acceptance that young Russian women should now be arriving in large numbers to ply their trade. But with

Which Way Next?

such a bleak economy at home, a new generation of girls is finding that the only way they can afford the trappings of the West is to, well, sell their most personal assets – or, to be perfectly accurate, to hire them out. Money can't buy you happiness, they always say, but it does at least allow you to rent it for a while.

Central European countries like Austria and Germany have long been used to Russian women competing for business alongside other working girls from the old Eastern Bloc.

But now, in places like Turkey, where Europe meets Asia, blonde and nubile Russian girls with their broad-shouldered minders are in conspicuous evidence at the larger hotels in resorts going east from Trabzon where the Black Sea coastline and road infrastructure is being improved at a rapid pace.

In Azerbaijan, too, where international businesses are developing links in the capital Baku on the prospects of an oil-rich future, Russian-born girls are readily available.

Strictly in the interests of research, a local contact took no more than 15 minutes on a mobile phone to summon up three attractive girls aged between 18 and 24 and to arrange a rendezvous in a convivial establishment of mock-Grecian décor fully equipped with massage tables, saunas and private accommodation.

Prices began at US$100, the equivalent of more than an average week's work in Russia, if jobs were available .

Euros, interestingly, which are now worth more than dollars, were also acceptable. But payment by American Express, a facility available at noticeably fewer establishments in Central Asia over the past year or two, was most definitely not.

- Richard Meredith, Central Asia, July 13 2003

APPENDIX 2

Georgian police get a capital idea

The policeman scribbles his price in pencil on the scrap of paper he pulls from his pocket: it will cost us US$80 if we want a "safe" passage over the next 45km of our journey. He doesn't have much English but he understands my protest that I think the price far too high. "OK, well you pay me US$20 now and ..." with a shrug of his shoulders he adds: "you can take your chances after that."

We have been driving in Georgia for precisely 25 minutes. Already we have been stopped by the police three times, just one or two of them stepping out into the road, blowing a whistle and waving us down. They want to look at our papers, they want to look at the car – and they want to pay their grocery bills.

We have done nothing wrong. Each time they want money, but I have managed to palm them off with cigarettes or some little knick-knack from the car. "We are from England, you see. We don't pay – won't pay – bribes to policemen," I explain.

But the fourth time is different. The unmarked car pulls in front of us and a man who says he's a cop asks for our passports. He is wearing what looks like an official visitors' badge and a gun. We hand over the passports, do as he gestures, and follow his car at rapid speed for another half mile until he deposits us into a clutch of three police cars and their occupants parked in a lay-by.

One of them soon explains the facts of life to me. He lays our map on the bonnet. "Where you going?"

I draw my finger up the line of the coast road.

"Police here. And here. And here," he says as he jabs his finger on the page. "You get much trouble, pay much money."

"And what if we go this way?" I make him understand that we could actually travel a different route.

"Ah, that way many Ali Babas. Boom, boom," he says cocking one hand like a gun and putting the other over his face in the pretence of a robber's mask.

Which Way Next?

It seems we have little choice. In this part of the former Soviet Union a new spirit of enterprise is flourishing – the police are going in for the escort agency business.

I negotiate the price down from US$80 to US$40, and as the chief cop climbs into our car I do what they do in the films and pay half to him now, telling him he gets the rest only when we get to where he says we will be safe from further instant road blocks or Ali Baba bandits.

And I hand it over too – after we have taken an hour to travel another 45km and passed through six more roadside police stops, where our escort uses his authority to wave aside all spurious claims of speeding or other traffic misdemeanours.

It was, in all the circumstances, probably a bargain. But that hardly seemed the point.

We had crossed into Georgia at the small border post of Sarpi after a good run along the Black Sea coastline of newly developing resorts in Turkey. The idea was – and still is – to make our way to Tbilisi, the Georgian capital, and then through Azerbaijan, across the Caspian, and on to Uzbekistan and Kazakhstan on a leg roughly following Marco Polo's legendary Silk Road.

But nothing we had read or heard prepared us for the highway robbery – and that is surely what it is – of the police in this south-western corner of Georgia.

We found that tourists and residents alike are being relieved of their money in a region stretching from Batumi to Poti – an area characterised by third world roads, empty tenement buildings and obviously high unemployment.

Just as obviously, the police issue no receipts. In our case, they offered no evidence of speeding or other accusations and appeared to have no technical equipment at all.

Payment is demanded in US dollars, and since they are armed there is also the fear of what could happen if we are tempted to ignore their signals to stop.

- Richard Meredith, Tbilisi, Georgia, July 11, 2003

APPENDIX 3

Nothing to declare but our wallets

We decided to go on a holiday with a difference this year. Actually, it wasn't so much of a holiday – it was more a cross between a beginner's guide to international officialdom and an endurance test. And we're still on it.

In June we left London and have so far driven across 22 countries to raise money for charity. That's been fine. But clearing the car through Customs has been an education.

Before we left, we discovered that the AA has abandoned its international carnet service and the RAC was soon to do the same. To be honest, we quite understand why. It's because inside borderless Europe it is largely unnecessary and outside of it, in our experience, it is pretty much a waste of time.

I had better explain.

We had set out on our marathon drive armed with an expensive RAC carnet. The carnet, an official document endorsed by international motoring associations, is intended to ease the pain of taking the car through Customs on entry and exit, and is meant to pay for itself by saving their fees.

But travelling east – apart from the odd exception – its jurisdiction essentially ends at Turkey. After that, it is either ignored or not recognised, and that's where the problems begin.

Perhaps not surprisingly, it is the countries of the former Soviet Union, where customs and practices have a long history of multi-layered bureaucracy, that are among the worst.

In Kazakhstan it took us a whole day (nine hours) to satisfy the Customs regulators, police and military that we were entitled to drive our car away from the port of Aqtau, where we had arrived on a ferry across the Caspian Sea.

It is the paperwork, not the car or its contents, which takes the time. All the officials insist it needs their stamp of approval, sometimes more than once – and there's usually a price to pay!

In Uzbekistan, where we arrived overnight sleeping in the car on a

Which Way Next?

flat-loading wagon at the back of a train, there was a different twist.

After loading the car, out in the wilds at a country station, someone had evidently tipped off the authorities that we wouldn't yet have any Customs papers. They stopped the train at 2.30am and imposed an on-the-spot fine of $50 (strictly cash and no receipts) despite our lengthy protests.

Going further east, the huge powers of Customs men to delay, approve or disapprove a shipment can be ... shall we say ...a big temptation to suggest financial lubrication.

In India we were told that a Customs official could retire after three years on the proceeds of back-handers from truck drivers and others who paid "dues" to speed their way through the system.

In Bangladesh, one of the most impoverished of nations, the government took the power of Customs clearance away from officers at their border crossings because of widespread corruption, and ordered that importers/exporters of cars like ours should report to designated offices before travelling.

Unfortunately we found that the scheme has only multiplied the problem, having been asked for "sweeteners" at both the offices *and* the border posts.

In Thailand there's another tale. They just impounded the car and held it for two weeks as we thumped our fists in frustration and waited helplessly as the storage and handling charges accumulated.

Nothing alters the physical inspection of the car and its contents for contraband goods, of course, but the carnet is meant to assure the authorities, through its detailed documentation, that the same car that enters the country also leaves it – and that it has not, for example, been sold for a substantial tax-free profit or been kitted out with fancy accessories at Third World prices.

The theory is fine – but in practice we concluded that it is the number of officials who get involved in the process, and the delays that ensue, which leads to the demand for queue-jumping ... by hook or by crook.

In Bangladesh for instance, it took seven separate signatures on a single sheet of paper from the Customs Revenue office before they would let us take our car out. And their country is actually one of the few signatories to the carnet system in Asia!

Mind you, there are sometimes happier stories to tell.

Beyond Tbilisi, at the border crossing into Azerbaijan, we grew so friendly with the Customs chief that he invited us to stop for tea and cakes. It turned out he was a devoted fan of British soccer and was keen to know the latest news and gossip.

Regrettably, all the talk of Beckham and Owen so took his mind off the task in hand that we later discovered he had put the wrong date on our entry papers, so that our time in his country had effectively finished before it began.

It took a bit of doing, but we escaped from that one too after a little no-receipt negotiating later.

- Richard Meredith, September 11, 2003

APPENDIX 4

Proud to help the children of Nepal

For a place that sits, quite literally, on top of the world, it has always seemed to me one of the most bitter of ironies that its people should fall so near to the bottom of it for prosperity.

Nepal is at once the most spectacular place. Perched right up there in the Himalayas, its land mass is squeezed between the borders of India, its hugely-populated neighbour to the south, and the Tibetan tongue of China.

There aren't many Nepalese. All of them could just about live in London, as a matter of fact. And they are very poor.

In one of the last assessments of these things, the average Nepalese family was found to have an income of something rather less than those in Malawi or Rwanda, countries where the problems of poverty are far wider publicised. Or, to put it another way, most people in western Europe will spend more in a week than a Nepalese family spends in a year.

Mostly they suffer in silence. The world does not hear much of the plight of those who are troubled by poor hygiene, inadequate education and a lack of basic living standards up there on the top of the world.

But the strange thing is, they still have smiles on their faces.

Maybe it is those mountains. Of the ten highest peaks in the world, Nepal has eight of them on or inside its borders: Everest, K2, Kanchenjunga, Annapurna … names so familiar to us all. And for those fortunate enough to have seen them, the experience will never be forgotten.

Adjectives become insufficient, because the majesty of their size and splendour is quite overwhelming. Look up at the clouds – and then imagine a mountain where the height of those clouds comes only halfway up it. Now you have some idea.

Perhaps that's the reason then; perhaps the very blessing of nature in setting such wondrous scenes in their midst is the reason why most of the Nepalese people I've met have a smile on their face – despite all their adversities.

I was there three years ago. It was my first time. I went round the triangle from Kathmandu, the dusty and overpopulated capital, to Chitwan, where we trampled our elephants through the jungle looking for tigers, and then to Pokhara, much higher up, trekking to the top of Sarangkot, still a mere goosebump by comparison to Mt Annapurna nearby.

It all left a lasting impression upon me – the memory of a proud, sallow-skinned race who lived their lives, like the children of Gulliver, in the shadow of giants, and who went about their daily lives as best they could, not so fearful of the consequences of tomorrow (though well they might) but happy for the inspirations of today.

What is so pleasing about the decision of SOS Children's Villages to donate money raised from the Daewoo Challenge towards building a new home for orphans in Nepal is that the benefits will help to keep those children smiling.

The charity is already doing much to assist this nation that one could say is an orphan itself. This year marks the 30th anniversary since families were able to move into the first SOS Children's Village in Sanothimi, close to Kathmandu. Now there are seven villages in Nepal, six youth facilities, seven schools, three training centres and a medical facility.

The new money will go towards another building at Bharatpur where 140 children will soon have a roof over their heads, food and clothing and education and – most important of all – a future to look forward to.

Work at the village, which has been financed to date mainly by the Austrian SOS Children's Villages association, is scheduled to finish in July and the first children will be able to move in by October.

We at the Daewoo Challenge team, feel very proud to know that our efforts will be helping in this wonderful project. And our message to those children – unlike so many orphans elsewhere – is that they are not forgotten.

- Richard Meredith, June 2003

APPENDIX 5
Nuts & Bolts

Reports, comments

Maintenance and repairs

Where/why	remark	remedy
Belgium/on-road check with prepping co.	internal fuel vapour	seal+ removing cowling
Paris/minor probs with master electronics	AC, fuel gauge etc., non-op	temporary cure
Rome/same	same	fixed
Athens/general check	exhaust loose at manifold	fixed
Tashkent/general check	tracking out	fixed
Delhi/general check	shocks shot	replaced
Bangkok/general check	MOT for customs	all OK
Hanoi/general check, esp.electronics	warning lights	fixed

Modifications

Under-body protection – a God-sent shield from rocks and flying debris

Strengthened suspension – an imperative for pot-holed,un-made roads and cart tracks

Extra fuel tank – a 'must' for more places in the world than you might think

Extra spots – excellent for picking out wandering cattle at night, pedestrians and unlit bicycles

Bull-bars – not needed, but certainly might have been

Steel walled tyres – remarkable (originals finished the trip)

Roof luggage box – watertight and indispensable for us

Verdict

Richard and Phil said: "Considering the Kalos is a regular family hatchback, our overall opinion of the Challenge car was that its performance and reliability were really outstanding. There were some electronic problems early on with the AC functioning only intermittently and the fuel gauges seemed to have a mind of their own. The suspension took a real hammering – especially in the second half from Central Asia going East – but it somehow held together. The shocks were replaced just before they came to bits and they needed doing again by the time we finished.

We monitored engine coolant, brake fluid, oil, battery and windscreen washer levels daily but the only topping-up they needed was at routine checks when they also took a look at the oil and air filters.

The power unit of 1.4 was often under strain – but that was hardly surprising with all that weight to pull (approx.1500kgs) and AC usage. On long or very hot journeys we tried to air the engine regularly with 10mins stops and we always aimed to keep the revs in the lower range.

Our interior storage was limited by spare tyres, the extra fuel tank, accessories box and all the bric-a-brac of travel, so the roof bubble really earned its keep.

Another plus was the adjustable steering wheel - ideal for two guys with approx. 6ins difference in height."

Printed in the United Kingdom
by BemroseBooth, Derby.